Hieroschemamonk

FEOFIL

Fool-For-Christ's-Sake

Ascetic and Visionary
Of The Kievo-Pecherskaya Lavra

Gathered and Compiled

by

VLADIMIR ZNOSKO

Printshop of St. Job of Pochaev
Holy Trinity Monastery
Jordanville, N.Y.
1998

Reprinted with the blessing
of
His Grace Laurus,
Archbishop of Syracuse and Holy Trinity Monastery

First Printing: 1970
Second Printing: 1987
Third Printing: 1998

HIEROSCHEMAMONK FEOFIL

TRANSLATORS' PREFACE

This translation of the book Hieroschemamonk Feofil *is slightly abridged in that most of the footnotes which appeared in the original have been blended into the text in this translation. The remainder of the footnotes appear at the end of the text.*

A definite effort was made to avoid corrupting the simplicity of the text with academic or "scholarly" rules and attitudes. The names of persons and places have been transliterated into English in a method which detracts least from the original Russian.

This book is the first of a series of such translations and the first rule which the translators adopted for this project was, in the words of the beloved Metropolitan Antony (Khrapovitsky), "There is no point in writing (religious works) for the intelligentsia because they will not read them anyway." It is better to write for the people who have not yet lost the desire to understand spiritual matters and to seek their salvation from Christ Jesus. They are the ones who are truly wise.

Translators' Introduction

The Blessed Starets Feofil departed from his earthly life more than one hundred and twenty-five years ago. Is it possible, then, that the example of his life, his teachings and admonitions, can still shine as a beacon-light to aid Christian people in this struggle along the narrow path which leads to salvation?

This book has been translated as a personal testimony by the translators, both of whom have been profoundly affected by the Blessed One, to the fact that Feofil is still very much an active starets. He does not limit himself to singing in the Church Triumphant; he is also a trusted intercessor and teacher for the Church Militant.

Aside from the rich spiritual joys presented in this biography of Starets Feofil, the book offers some rare and valuable insights into the personality of Tsar Nikolai Pavlovich and the saintly Metropolitan Filaret of Kiev. Moreover, the mentality of Old Russia is reflected on every page. In fact, no student of Russian history or culture can claim even a superficial knowledge of his subject unless he has studied the lives of the great saints and ascetics of the Russian Orthodox Church, for the lives and minds of the Russian people have always been welded to the blessed refuge of the Church.

We address a special prayer of thanksgiving to God that He, in His infinite mercy, has given us such candles as Feofil. May all who read this book approach it with mind and heart open for instruction and love.

Glory to Thee, O God!

PREFACE

The Blessed Starets, Hieroschemamonk Feofil, is so popular amongst Kievans and many other Orthodox Christians that, although he demised long ago, his memory remains sacredly and reverently honoured.

It is true that none of his contemporaries who witnessed his monastic podvigs, his life as a fool-for-Christ's-sake, and spiritual glory are still alive. But, amongst the descendants of these people, many recollections of the God-pleasing life and gift of forevision of the Blessed One are passed down from one generation to another.

For more than thirty years the Starets served as a bright lamp of Evangelical truth for all Orthodox Christians and he was the best example of monkhood at the Kiev-Pecherskaya Lavra for a decade.

As a great teacher of piety, he worked at the improvement of the morals of those nearest him ... **warning and admonishing everyone and instructing everyone in all wisdom, that we may present every person mature in Christ, the Anointed One** (Col. 1:28).

By means of spiritual eyes which penetrated the innermost recesses of men's hearts, the Blessed Feofil saw much. He saw how pride, self-delusion, hatred and violence inhabited the darkness of our ignorance. He saw how, plunging into a chaos of passions not penetrated by a single ray of divine light, people forgot God and, being satiated with sins, became filled with material food but starved for spiritual nourishment — Christians in name only, but in deeds and life, far from it.

Starets Feofil saw much and secretly suffered for all souls. In order to support the failing spirit of faith in us, he, out of love, took upon himself the highest podvig of Christian piety — being a fool-for-Christ's-sake. He dedicated his whole life to the doctoring of moral ailments. Using parables, he sternly revealed cruel and unjust people who had forgotten God. With meek reproof and with kindness he comforted and encouraged believing and God-fearing people. **God in His wisdom was pleased through the foolishness of preaching to save those who believed** (I Cor. 1:21).

Out of true piety and love of God, Feofil refused temporary blessings and led his entire life in humility, simplicity, and abasement. He experienced defamation, insult, evil, and hatred from people but, being humble of heart and meek in spirit, he did not even complain to the Lord about his critics, limiting himself only to the prayer uttered on the cross by the Great Sufferer: **"Father, forgive them for they know not what they do"** (Luke 23:34).

His memory will not depart and his name will live from generation to generation. People will know of his wisdom and the Church will proclaim his praise.

The descendants of people who knew the Blessed Starets have reverently preserved a multitude of remembrances about **his wonderful forevision** and the effectiveness of his prayers for those suffering and burdened with ailments of the body and the spirit.

We offer here to the reader only a few of them, collected during interviews with the elder residents of Kiev or given to us by the God-loving startsy of the Kiev-Pecherskaya Lavra.'

We will not hide these things, but will present them for all to see; may the light of the Blessed Starets Feofil appear as a beacon and may he illumine the world with his deeds which in his lifetime the world did not understand, seeing in the man of God nothing but foolishness.

I

In the town of Makhnovo, district of Kiev, at the Church of the Birth of the Virgin, there once lived a priest, Andrei Gorenkovsky. In October, 1788, his wife Evfrosiniya (nee Goshkovsky) gave birth to twins. At baptism the eldest was named Foma and the younger, Kalliniky. They were both notably beautiful and strong.

It was the custom at that time for mothers to breast-feed their own infants. Evfrosiniya abided by this rule even though it was quite difficult with two children involved. She refused all offers of assistance from wet nurses. To her great amazement, however, Evfrosiniya found that her eldest son, Foma, would not take to the breast, stubbornly averting his face from it. In order to save the child from starving to death, the distressea mother was forced to try every possible means of feeding him. Since he refused all forms of milk, his mother fed him with potato water, soft-boiled turnips and carrots.

Such a rejection from her child naturally settled a coldness in the mother's heart towards the baby. To make matters worse, superstitious neighborhood women began interpreting this phenomenon in their own way and dragging in absurd stories, considering Foma to be almost a bear-cub.

Evfrosiniya, because of her own simpleness and ignorance, believed from her soul all these superstitious tales. She became horrified and her bitterness towards Foma grew. "This is an exchange," she would say. "They did not want to baptise him and Kalliniky on the same day and so a witch substituted him."

Evfrosiniya tried for six months, by all possible means, to make Foma behave like a normal child. But all the while she saw in him the embryo of some sort of inclinations, incomprehensible to the simple woman. Deciding that Foma was some sort of moral freak, Evfrosiniya resolved to rid herself of him forever. One evening she called a servant and secretly confided in her:

"I can no longer look at this vampire; I cannot stand him in my own home. Tomorrow, at the very crack of dawn, take him to the river and throw him into it. But swear to me that no-one will know about this except us."

The servant begged and pleaded with the mother to have mercy on the innocent child. No matter how much she pleaded and wept, admonishing Evfrosiniya with God's wrath, the embittered mother was implacable. In the end, the servant had to submit to her.

In the morning, when it was barely light, the servant took Foma in her arms, ran to the river and, making a sign of the cross over the child, dropped him into the water. And then a wondrous thing happened. God chose to preserve the child. He came up to the surface of the water and peacefully floated to the opposite shore. There he was cast up onto the dry ground.

On seeing this, the servant became terrified. Having already committed a crime and fearing the wrath of her mistress, she decided to bring the terrible matter to a swift end. She crossed the stream and picked up Foma in her arms. The child was asleep in a serene slumber. Then, avoiding thought, the servant quickly dropped the baby into the river once more. Again she witnessed God's power; the waves carried Foma to a little island which had been formed upstream and gently cast him up on the fine sand.

Shaken by such an undeniable miracle, the woman crossed a ford and took the child in her arms. Seeing that the baby was alive and unharmed, the servant was flooded with bitter tears of repentance. She took Foma to his mother and, in a voice choked with fear, related to her all that had happened.

"You can kill me, but I will not drown an innocent child! God Himself, by a miracle, is saving his life and we shall suffer for our cruel murder!"

But the young mother, compelled by an inhuman bitterness, did not believe a word the servant said and began to reproach her. "Shame on you!" she said. "You are pitying this vampire. If we leave him alive, he will bring about much evil. Oh no! It may be better that I drown him with my own hands than to look at this freak which is hateful to my sight."

With these words, Evfrosiniya maliciously seized Foma from the arms of the frightened servant woman and set out for the river. Not far from their home stood a water mill. Since it was early and no-one was around, Evfrosiniya approached it, found an appropriate spot and, with a great swing, threw Foma under the wheel itself. Then, thinking that the child was dead, she left. Her conscience seemed peaceful. Then suddenly there was another miracle. The millstones stopped and the pressure of the water caused a tremendous roar.

The miller, startled by the strange phenomenon, ran outside to see what had happened. The wheels, restrained by an unknown power, trembled from the strong pressure of the water driving against them. The water raged ahead, foaming and boiling. Looking down, he heard an infant's wails and in the midst of the whirlpool he saw the child floating. Then the miller nimbly lowered himself down and, bending towards the stream, pulled Foma out of the water. Hardly had he removed the child than the wheels began to turn again.

The distraught servant who had followed the desperate mother, seeing this new miracle, began sobbing bitterly. She approached the miller and related all that she knew about the child and about the miraculous phenomena of God's power which had saved the child thrice.

"What shall we do now?" puzzled the miller. "If we return the babe to his mother, she will not hesitate to destroy him."

Fearing responsibility for the fate of the innocent child persecuted by his own mother, they decided to relate these incidents to his father.

Neither pleas nor prayers, nor even threats and coercion had any effect upon Evfrosiniya. In the constant saving of the child, she saw only the devil's work. The more that the husband tried to convince her, the more stubborn she became.

"I will not leave him alive. This is not a little child. This is an exchange, a freak. He definitely must be freed of life," repeated the superstitious Evfrosiniya and tried several more times to destroy Foma.

The heart-broken father, seeing how strongly his wife hated her own son, decided to take Foma away from her for a long time. He secretly sought out an experienced wet-nurse and told her the details of the family secret, and gave her the innocent child to be brought up. The hired nurse fed Foma with soft bread soaked in fat and gave daily reports on her charge to the father.

Several months passed and the child developed normally and even strengthened. The wet-nurse proved to be a woman of good conscience. She raised and cared for Foma as she would her own son. But soon God found it pleasing to call Foma's father from temporary life to eternal. Feeling the approach of his death, the priest, filled with concern for the future of his son, called the good miller to himself and said:

"You were a witness to the miraculous saving of my child. In the name of God I entrust you to take Foma to yourself. Raise him, guard him, and do not offend him."

With joy the miller agreed, accepting his charge as a blessing from God.

Meanwhile, the story of these happenings had spread amongst the people of the district. A wealthy old peasant from the town of Makhnovo came to the miller and begged for the guardianship of the child.

"I have no children," he said, "and I want to make this child my son and after my death I will make him heir to all I possess. Let me have Foma."

The miller, seeing the sincerity of the old peasant, gave in to his persistent requests and, without any vacillation, handed Foma over to him. It was a happy time for the child, living under the shelter of the wealthy man. He was treated with tenderness and love. In time, Foma would become a son and also rich. So it would have been if human plans always agreed with the paths of God's providence. But the Lord moved otherwise. Not long after Foma was embraced into the family of the rich peasant, the benefactor and second father suddenly, without expectation, died.

And so the persecuted child, not yet three years of age, again became an orphan.

The wife of the deceased peasant came into full possession of his estate. Having resolved to take a second husband, she hurriedly set about finding other quarters for Foma. The priest of her own village compassionately accepted the child.

"He is binding my hands," the widow justified herself, "and you, Batiushka, can easily lead him along that road which is more becoming to his position as son of a priest."

Agreement was made and little Foma found himself in a new refuge. Thus, from his earliest days, he became acquainted with the spirit of a wandering life. Being yet a new-comer to this life, Foma had already taken upon himself the cross of Him Who, during His life on earth, did not have a place to lay His head.

Foma lived with his guardian until the age of seven. There was no special attention shown him and the priest did not present him with any deliberate instruction. Foma, left to himself, unwillingly took part in the noisy games with children his own age. To the surprise of all, the young lad showed no desire for the usual entertainments of his age group. Foma preferred to go aside to an isolated place and give himself up to melancholy meditation.

Little Foma was accustomed to the wandering spirit. He experienced the sweetness of a child's first prayers to his very soul. Early in life he became used to lengthy fasting and frugality. Gradually he strengthened and became spiritually transformed. God's temple became the dearest refuge of this unusual child. The boy would not miss a single service and, with the first peel of the bell he hurried with great joy to the church where his soul found comfort and incomprehensible rest. Foma was often found before the closed doors of the village church, deep in prayer, as if severed from all his surroundings.

The other children, seeing Foma's closed soul, mocked him and made fun of him; he was often subjected to tricks and even beatings. Foma would go away into the woods, weeping, and remain there for twenty-four, or even forty-eight, hours at a time. Often he would be found by shepherds who would relate wonderful stories about him. The young sufferer understood that man is not born to joy and happiness but to suffering.

Having himself experienced all the bitterness of his young life, he could see that the world often does not behold sufferers; it does not see the tears of the eyes. From his early youth Foma discovered the joy of aiding those in poverty. He refused to keep things for himself and gave all that he possibly could to the poor. Once Foma saw another boy in the street wearing only old rags in place of a shirt. Without even a second thought, he removed his own shirt and gave it to the poor boy, returning home in only his outer garments. His benefactor looked at this differently and Foma received only punishment for his podvig of charity.

When Foma reached the age of seven, the priest began teaching him to read. But soon after, the priest died and so, with the demise of the good teacher, the young wanderer again became homeless. Foma wept bitterly and inconsolably for his benefactor. He wept less for his loss of a home than for the loss of a wise teacher, who had barely begun to open the world of learning and wisdom to him.

After the death of the priest, it was necessary to find a new refuge for Foma. The elder of the church, assuming that after a seven-year period the former hatred towards her son would have disappeared from Evfrosiniya and that she would now feel a maternal tenderness for him, decided to take Foma back home. When the elder arrived at the home of Evfrosiniya, she was splitting wood. How great was the horror and astonishment of the old man when, instead of receiving her son with love, the mother threw her axe at him in a rage so that the blade of the axe cleaved into Foma's right shoulder.

The elder quickly seized the bleeding child from the grasp of his maddened mother, bound his wound, and took Foma back to his own home. While Foma's wound was healing, the elder discovered that an uncle of the boy was a widowed priest living as a starets at the Bratsky Monastery in Kiev. The kindly elder took the child, not yet healed, to this monk. There, he related to the starets all that he knew about the unfortunate nephew and handed over the boy to be brought up.

There is an ecclesiastical academy at the Bratsky Monastery and at that time there were beginners' classes. The much-suffering orphan was assigned to this academy and there began to acquire the wisdom of books.

Taking advantage of his uncle's hospitable refuge, Foma grew up in model behaviour and studied hard. In his spare moments he devoted himself to the reading of theological books and solitary praying. He understood the psalms well and derived much comfort and joy from memorising them.

The pure, child's prayers of Foma were pleasing to God and He softened the heart of the cruel mother and caused a reconciliation between Evfrosiniya and her repudiated son.

This wonderful event took place thus:

Evfrosiniya was stricken with an incurable illness. Seeing the punishment of the Lord upon her, she began tearfully to repent of her cruelties and persecutions of the innocent son. No matter how hard she tried she could not find peace with herself. During the day her ailment tortured her and at night she was tormented with nightmares. In this she saw God's justice. All the while her meek son wept and prayed for her. Finally, the mother understood her terrible error and began to beg God for His forgiveness. The Lord pitied her. Not long before her death Foma came home to his mother and each had the consolation of a re-union.

"Forgive me, my son," the repentant mother cried out to Foma. "Forgive me, cruel, foolish, terrible that I am. My mind was in darkness and I did not see the great evil created by me. May God's blessings be upon you. Do not curse me, an evil mother, and remember me, a sinner, in your constant prayers."

With these words Evfrosiniya pressed her son tightly against her maternal breast and, making the sign of the cross upon him, she quietly released her soul. The good Foma closed her life-less eyes with his own hands and handed over the body of his mother for burial.

II

Foma was an excellent student at the academy but he had no inclination to continue his higher academic studies. He could not accept them as a true means of acquiring that knowledge which leads to the truth of God and His grandeur. Foma chose the Church as his highest school. He dedicated himself to reading and singing and disciplined his mind to constant spiritual thought and prayer. From this time, thoughts about monkhood never left him for a moment and he aimed his goals towards that end.

Foma's good uncle died after a short time and left his nephew with no means of livelihood and without a true shelter. There was no longer any thought of continuing his studies. He left the academy and began to earn his own livelihood. In 1810 he went to the town of Chigirin as a reader but, because his voice was quite poor, he was sent to the village of Obukhov as a sacristan.

Foma did not remain there long. The world, which had not liked him since his birth, oppressed him with its rules and laws, and turned his soul away from itself. **"My soul longeth, yea,"** Foma said, **"even fainteth for the courts of the Lord"** (Ps. 84:2). Conceiving a deep dislike for the mass of evil-intented and dishonourable people, Foma entered the Kiev Bratsky Monastery in 1812, in the very heat of the "Patriotic War."

What unrelatable joy filled the young ascetic. He once more had entered the holy place of the quiet cloister which he had left two years earlier. This time not for study but for prayer, patience, toil, and fasting. He was dead to the world and the world died for him forever.

In the Bratsky Monastery, Foma fulfilled various obediences. He mixed dough and baked bread in the bakery but at that time, prosphora were not baked at the Bratsky Monastery and Foma used to go for them to the Florovsky Monastery for women. Later, he was assigned to the kitchen to make borshch. Then he was appointed assistant in the hospital and finally sacristan and bell-ringer. He especially liked this latter task. At the break of dawn he would rise, go up into the belfry and give himself up to deep contemplation and secret prayer. No-one bothered him here. The vain world lay at his feet and in front of his gaze, in all its splendour, he could see only the azure heaven where the Creator of all things visible and invisible dwelt.

In this way several years passed. Redoubling his prayerful podvigs, Foma appeared to everyone as an example of meekness, obedience, humility, and chastity. With all his soul he desired a rank equal to the angels. He constantly repeated, **"I have longed for Thy salvation, O Lord; and Thy law is my delight"** (Ps. 119:174).

Foma did not press the matter of his tonsure, which was his heart's desire, wishing first to teach himself the strict implementation of the rules of monastic living. Nevertheless, the head of the monastery noticed in him a fervour towards spiritual podvigs, and honoured Foma with his tonsure on 11 December, 1821. At the time of his tonsure, Foma was renamed Feodorit.

Soon after this Feodorit was appointed keeper of the vestments and on 30 September, 1822, because of his dedication to work in that position and because of his exemplary, strictly monastic life, he was elevated to the rank of hierodeacon.

The new position gave a new thrust to his podvigs. Now able to stand closer to the altar of the King of Glory, Feodorit, with all his strength, tried to imitate the angelic lives of those who had already pleased God and now faced the heavenly throne of the Lamb, Who took on Himself the sins of the entire world. According to his position, Feodorit received a small income but remained a stern faster and had nothing personal in his cell. On the contrary, he was a stranger to acquiring things and even found in this income the means to be charitable to his near ones. Remaining without food for two or three days at a time, he gave away his share of food and money to wanderers, the poor, and to beggars.

"What is it to me, this flesh and blood, which one day will turn to dust," Feodorit would say and then redouble his fasting.

He showed a God-imitating love for those near him and willingly fulfilled obediences to those in the lowest order, often taking upon himself the work of others, serving like a bought slave. In this way he followed in the footsteps of the Saviour Himself Who came ... **not to be served but to serve** (Matt. 20:28).

On 6 February, 1827, Feodorit was ordained hieromonk and at the same time appointed steward of the Bratsky Monastery. This rank was bestowed as an honour at the monastery and was greatly desired by many. The position was very solicitious and did not at all correspond to the sincere inclinations of Hieromonk Feodorit. In order to avoid meeting people and preferring to remain in complete isolation, he promptly requested to be released from the stewardship and refused all obediences. He asked for permission to retire to the caves which had been dug by Saint Feodosy in the village of Lesniky. Having been refused this, Feodorit took the path of special asceticism and took upon himself the great podvig of "fool-for-Christ's sake." In his feigned eccentricity he concealed the high valour of his character.

He continued to rise from strength to strength in the difficult matter of his spiritual improvement. Thus, Feodorit followed the words of the apostle who said, **If any man among you supposes that he is wise in the world... let him become a fool so that he may become truly wise** (I Cor. 3:18).

Now he had less striving for spiritual improvement because **the Lord had already tried his heart and knew his thoughts** (Ps. 139:23). From his childhood Feodorit was gifted with humility and spiritual purity. He had a strong faith in the help of God Who extracted him from the path of the sand and marsh and set his feet upon solid rock, strengthening his steps. Feodorit could say, in truth, **"My heart is ready O Lord, my heart is ready!"** Having set his feet upon the highest podvig of the monastic life, Feodorit, on 9 December, 1834, took the schema (monastic habit) and was re-named Feofil.

For the ordinary monk the schema is an image of bodily death and a struggling upward to ascend into eternity. For the Blessed Feofil, who had prepared himself for the service of God from the first days of his life, it became a sign of the complete repudiation of the world and a spiritual transference to heaven. Death, judgment, and the kingdom — this is what now occupied his thoughts and all the hours of his contemplation.

It was with joy that the Blessed Feofil set out on this narrow and sorrowful path so that, by travelling on it, he could reach the serene state of freedom from the passions of the flesh. Now he was a true warrior of Christ, invested with all of God's weapons against all of mankind's weaknesses and temptations. A stranger to all that is worldly vanity, he disregarded all the conditions of daily life. Feofil did not develop close relationships with anyone and completely closed the temple of his soul from the world which did not like him even from his infancy. Only prayer opened his lips and praises to the Creator moved his tongue.

With lowered eyes, he always walked peacefully, deep in thought, along the usual path from his cell to the church, never missing a single service. Stopping either at the entrance or near the church doors which were often closed, he stood motionless to the end of the service. Near him there was always a basket filled with various provisions to be given to those who needed them. He always carried a bucket, bowl, or jug and a small Psalter.

Having increased his podvig of foolishness even more, the Blessed One placed an old coffin in his cell but did not lie in it at night as did many of the ancient ascetics of piety but he kept various provisions and dishes in it. Moreover, on the day of his tonsuring to the schema, Feofil sewed pieces of old rags around his cowl and wore it that way until his death. When these shreds were ripped off on the day of his death, the cowl appeared new and fit for burial.

Every morning the Starets would set out for the Dniepr where he went to get water. At times he would get into one of the boats moored nearby and row to the opposite shore of the Dniepr where, entering into the depths of the woods, he gave himself up to the contemplation of God. He never sought ferry-men but took any boat he happened to see and rowed himself across the river. The owners knew of Feofil's habits and never worried about their missing boats. They never prevented him from doing what he wanted; to the contrary, they even rejoiced if he took their boat.

As a zealous carrier of Divine Grace and gifts of the Holy Spirit, the Blessed Feofil did not conceal himself from the attention and reverence of the people. They used to step back from him in a circle and followed him everywhere in the hope of hearing even a single word from him. Thus the Lord places the lowly on the heights. But the academy authorities had no special sympathy for "the dirty, ragged monk Feofil" and complained constantly about him to the Vladika, pointing out that crowds of curious people searched for Feofil and blocked off the academy, even entering the buildings, destroying silence, and disrupting the pupils' studies. Because of these complaints, the Blessed One received strong reproof and, in order to avoid more difficulty, he found it necessary to hide in the woods from his followers, returning home only after sunset. But even then the crowds of people found him and waited for him on the shore of the Dniepr following him all the way to his cell.

As a result of his zeal, diligence, and flaming love of the Crucified One, God illumined Feofil with the light of heavenly wisdom so that everything secret and incomprehensible in the moral-physical nature was natural, possible, and comprehensible for the Starets. The Blessed Feofil predicted with accuracy not only all the phenomena of the visible world but also all that was hidden in the depths of man's heart. It is said that the grace of God began to appear in Feofil in his very early days while he was still a postulant-sacristan.

In Feofil's time, it was the custom of the sisters of the Florovsky Monastery to go to the Dniepr for water every day. The river water had a high iron content and was healthier and purer than well water. The shortest path to the Dniepr lay through the grounds of the Bratsky Monastery and this was the route taken by the sisters. It was a rule, however, that no postulant could leave the gates of the monastery without the blessing of her staritsa. All those who set out for the river for water were obliged to inform their nearest superior. In spite of this decree, it happened that one of the young postulants, taking advantage of the absence of the staritsa from her cell, went to the Dniepr for water without the required blessing. She came to the river and was just about to dip in her bucket when she lost her balance and dropped her cell key, which she had been holding in her hand, into the water. In her great confusion the poor soul began to sob and wring her hands. How could she present herself to her staritsa? She could not open her locked cell and she would have to explain the loss of the key. Suddenly, from somewhere or other, Blessed Feofil appeared.

"Why are you weeping?" he asked. The young girl told him her grief. "It serves you right, silly. The next time you won't go without a blessing. However, give me the bucket and I will help you."

The postulant handed him the bucket. The Blessed One stooped towards the river and, having made a sign of the cross on the vessel, he scooped up a full bucket.

"Here, take it and go home. Here you have both water and the lost key."

The postulant looked into the bucket and saw her lost key on the bottom. With a joyful cry of gratitude the young girl rushed after Feofil but his footsteps had already vanished.

And so, amazing everyone with the greatness of his spirit and life, the Blessed Feofil was a living testimony of the wonderful strength of the nature of mankind; what kind of power and might are confined in the soul and body of man, if only man will strive to be thoroughly penetrated by the strength and might of Christ's grace.

A naive peasant who was curious to know why the Blessed One could foretell the future and penetrate the innermost parts of man's heart, stepped up to him and asked:

"Father, how is it that you know everything and can foretell the future of people's lives?"

"There is nothing difficult about it," the Blessed One replied.

"Could it really be so simple, Father?" the peasant asked.

"Very simple. Do you want to be able to do the same?"

"Very much so, Father; teach me."

"Well then," instructed Feofil, "pull a small hair from your eyelash and tie two knots in it. When you do that you will be as wise as I am."

"Do you mean that you attained this by such means?"

"Indeed," replied Starets Feofil.

The naive peasant tried to make use of this advice but no matter how hard he tried, he could not even tie one knot in the eyelash.

"That is how difficult it was for me to attain my present condition," said the Blessed One and turned away from the peasant.

Many pupils of the academy, in order to tempt the Blessed One, tried to find him in his cell and converse with him on the subject of spiritual education. They were, however, struck by his simple and wise answers. They were amazed that such a sullen-appearing and untidy schemamonk could expose their thoughts by his sharp expressions. When the more impudent turned the conversation to make mockery, the Blessed One, desiring to end the useless visit, would sharply break them off:

"Go away from me! There was a time when I studied but now my mind has become dark. If I continue to talk to you, perhaps, for all I know, you might knock me off the true path. Go, go! For it is written in the Scriptures **'But refuse to have anything to do with trifling controversies over ignorant questionings for you know that they foster strife and breed quarrels'.**" (2 Tim. 2:23).

But it cannot be said that all scoffed at the Blessed One. There were occasions when the example of the great ascetic was imitated. At the very beginning of his podvigs as a fool-for-Christ's-sake, there was a student of the academy, one Pyotr Gavrilovich Kryzhanovsky. Feofil was still a postulant when a brotherly friendship tied them together. The young friends spent whole hours in soul-saving talks, discussing the fate of mankind, worldly vanity, and fate beyond the grave. The Blessed Feofil saw good strivings and a sympathetic heart in his friend and tried by all means to strengthen and increase these good seeds of God's word in his soul.

"**Acquaint now yourself with Him,**" Feofil would say to his friend, "**and be at peace; thereby good shall come to you. Receive, I beseech you, the law from His mouth, and lay up His words in your heart!** (Job 22, 21:22). And if you fulfill your vows **the light shall shine on your ways** (Job 22:28)."

These constant talks created a beneficial influence on the young Pyotr. Impressionable by nature, Pyotr began to meditate and vigilantly took measure of his friend. He could not live without him for a minute. Once they met on the shore of the Dniepr and, sitting down next to each other on the grass, they began to talk.

"My brother! Help me to save my soul," cried Pyotr, turning to Feofil.

"You can do this alone," replied the Blessed One, "as long as there is the desire and the zeal."

"How can I do it? Teach me."

"Repudiate the world and all that is in it; close the innermost part of your soul to everyone; crucify your flesh together with passions and lust and, finding yourself in incessant prayer, select a narrow path which leads to eternal life."

"I swear to God," replied Pyotr, "I am prepared to do what you order me but due to my inexperience and simpleness, it will be difficult for me to attain the desired success."

"Then walk in my footsteps and imitate my podvigs and you will be saved."

From that time, young Pyotr seemed to be completely transformed. He became silent and contemplative, no longer joking or laughing and he abruptly changed his way of living. He would spend entire days sitting over his books, or else spending all his time in God's temple and he began to fast zealously. The academy superiors noticed this sudden change in Pyotr and they began to observe him. They attempted to administer strict reproofs to him but nothing mattered. Disregarding worldly rules and customs, Pyotr seemed to be scolding the world. Eventually, Pyotr became disturbed by the authorities' constant watching of him so he chose the grounds of the Florovsky Monastery as a place for his solitary podvigs. There he spent many hours in solitude, seeking some empty corner so that he could sink into prayer. It once happened that Pyotr remained past the hour when the gates were locked and he was trapped within the cloister. In order to conceal himself, he went into the monastery cellar, lighted a candle and began to read the Holy Gospel. Some of the sisters came there for provisions and upon seeing such an unusual sight, they became frightened and raised a clamour. A whole throng came running. Abbess Serafima came to the place of the incident, but the matter was explained, settled, and ended with Pyotr being sent away from the monastery.

"Why do you do this?" Pyotr was asked on the following day by his uncle, Father Andrei Stefanovsky, a priest of the Florovsky Monastery. "Why don't you stay in the Bratsky Monastery and study or else you will discredit my name and harm yourself."

But Pyotr remained silent and did not respond. Only when he would lose courage and his soul would become seized by despondency, he would run for advice to his teacher and fall sobbing on Feofil's breast.

"Restrain yourself; restrain yourself," the Blessed One would console his faint-hearted friend. "**Take your share of the hardships and suffering as a good soldier of Jesus Christ** (2 Tim. 2:3). ... **That enemy of yours, the devil, roams around like a lion roaring hungrily, looking for someone to seize upon and devour** (1 Pet. 5:8). Don't be frightened by your podvig and lead it to its end. It is difficult but through it you will avoid the fire of Gehenna. If your hands are cramped from toil, just wash them with prayer to God and let your feet follow after prayer. ... **unless a grain of wheat falls into the earth and dies, it remains just one grain, alive but by itself. But if it dies, it produces many others and yields a rich harvest** (John 12:24). And so, if you want to be fruit-bearing, die in your present image so that you can carry in your heart the feeling that you have already died."

"But believe me, that it is difficult for me. My strength has run altogether low. My relatives do not understand me and with their cries they torment my heart and upset my mind."

"Do not listen to them; behave like a dead person who does not respond to anything surrounding hm. If you are praised — be silent. If you are scolded — be silent. If you incur losses — be silent. If you receive profit — be silent. If you are satiated — be silent. If you are hungry — also be silent. And do not be afraid that there will be no fruit when all dies down; there will be! Not everything will die down. Energy will appear — and what energy!"

Heeding the directions of his spiritual adviser, Pyotr would again revive in spirit and redouble his podvigs. Soon this young ascetic was excluded from the academy. His relatives, not comprehending the secret of his elevated spirit, committed Pyotr to the Kirillovskaya Mental Hospital. He remained there for nearly eight years but never once left his podvig of fool-for-Christ's sake. He reached such a high spiritual perfection that he even foretold his own death. Not long before his demise, Pyotr left the hospital, clad only in a dressing gown, and went to the Florovsky Monastery to bid farewell to the sisters.

"Farewell, you who have become Christ's bride. Tomorrow we shall see each other no more."

Pyotr was soon seized by hospital attendants who had followed him to the monastery and returned to Kyrillovskaya. On the following day Pyotr died and thus remained an enigma to all who knew him well.

On the day of Pyotr's death, Starets Feofil was at the Kitayevskaya Hermitage and he sent one of the sisters of the Florovsky Monastery to pay his last respects to his deceased friend. He instructed her:

"Go, cast your eyes on him and lower your head to him who was patient and strong in spirit. That is how all who believe in Him and love Him are saved. For truthful is the word of the Lord which says ... **if we have died with Him, we shall also live with Him. If we endure, we shall also reign with Him** (2 Tim. 2:11-12)."

Feofil became tired of the noisy life of the Bratsky Monastery and began to think about finding a more suitable place for his solitary podvigs. For this purpose he selected a large and shady orchard in Glubochitsa where the Pokrovsky Monastery now stands. The owner of this orchard, Iosif Nikiforovich

Dikovsky, respected the Starets and always sought his advice and directions. Because he was under the influence of the Blessed One, Dikovsky led a truly ascetic life. He slept little, fasted, did not eat meat, prayed much, and occupied Himself with the reading of soul-saving books.

Nazar, the son of Iosif Dikovsky, who is today (1906) ninety years old, relates: "Starets Feofil used to come to our orchard and hurry to his bees. He had only a few beehives, three or four, but he used to look after them with fatherly attention. And how healthy they were! Not a single one of them ever died of illness. He was very fond of me. He would see me in the orchard and cry out, 'Nazar, come here!' I would go to him and ask for his blessings. 'God gives His blessings. Are you still catching fish? Catch some for me and the two of us will make some fish soup.' We had a pond in our orchard with huge carp in it. I would catch some for the Starets and he would place it, raw, into his basket. Whenever he came he would always reproach me, 'Why don't you marry, Nazar?' 'I am young, Father.' But I was over twenty-seven then. Take care, get married, or else you will have no-one to lead you by your hand in your old age.' 'But whom shall I marry, Father? I don't love or even know anyone.' 'The baker woman, Nazar. She will go after you.' I, of course, would laugh, 'And which baker woman? I haven't even seen a bread basket since I was born.' Unfortunately, my father overheard our conversation and he, too, began to pressure me into marriage. There was no way out so I had to marry. And with whom do you think I joined my fate?

With a baker woman! Evfrosinya Kagarlitskaya was her name. Her mother was a poor woman who baked bread and sold it in the market. And I never saw her once before the wedding. It was just before the crowning that I found out everything. I asked my wife, 'What did you and your mother do?' 'We baked bread.' 'That's how you made your living?' 'Yes, with the prayers of Father Feofil we had quite good sales.' 'Do you mean to say that he knew you?' 'Of course he knew us. He used to send someone from the Bratsky Monastery to my mother, Ustina. He would have the messenger tell my mother, a widow, to send some rolls and if there were none, to give some raw dough. Only God knows why he needed the dough. It would seem that he gave it away with prophecies to his visitors. And what an income we would have that day! Mother would always sell every last roll at the market.'

I have been paralyzed for thirteen years now. I can neither walk nor dress without someone's help. My wife looks after me like a little child. Only now did the words of the Blessed Visionary Feofil come to mind: 'Get married, Nazar, or else you will have no-one to lead you by the hand in your old age.'

The Starets did not travel by carriage but on a little horse. At that time there was a merchant by the name of Ivan Katkov living in Podol. He very much honoured and feared the Blessed One and he made him a gift of a little horse. The Starets could not care for the animal in the monastery, so Katkov would send it to Father Feofil each day already fed and watered. The Starets would hitch the horse to a little wagon, seat himself in it, and read his Psalter along the way. The horse walked along unguided. As he went down the road, street urchins would seek to annoy him. Often a whole throng would run after him crying, 'Feofil, Feofil, take us with you!' Sometimes one would even throw a stone at him. The Starets would only glance at the rude one, shake his finger at him sternly, and again lower his eyes to his Psalter."

Iosif Dikovsky was not the only one close to the heart of the Starets. Feofil loved his whole family. Dikovsky's eldest daughter was married to a cattle dealer, Ivan Grigorievich Rudkin. Reverently honouring the Blessed Starets, Rudkin did not take on any matters without his advice and blessings. Even when preparing to set out for the fair, he first went to Kitayev for the Starets' blessings before setting out on his way. Once Evgeniya came to Father Feofil on some matter and the Starets asked her, "Why, oh servant of God, do you not marry off your children?"

"I can't find any bridegrooms, Father."

"Can't find any bridegrooms? Well then, take care, it will be bad for your soul when it becomes necessary to cross the flaming river."

"But you will extend your cane, Father, and I will cross," she replied jokingly.

The Starets went into his cell and brought out a piece of white bread spread with black fish roe.

"Here is something for you. Don't be afraid, take it. And as soon as you return home give it to your daughter. She will soon marry a famous person."

After some time had passed, the Rudkins' daughter was betrothed and wed to Professor Konstantin Skvortsov.

On another occasion, Rudkina again came to the starets on some matter. As she was preparing to leave, she said, "Father, how is it that you have completely forgotten my father? Come and visit him. See how nice our orchard is now."

"I'll come, I'll come," the Starets replied tenderly.

And very soon he did arrive at their place in Glubochitsa. The Blessed One's meeting with Dikovsky was extremely touching. Iosif Nikiforovich had not seen the Starets for several years and, rejoicing like a child, began to show the Starets various improvements on his property.

"Nice, very nice," the Blessed One said. "It has blossomed beautifully."

Later, while strolling in the orchard with Dikovsky, they stopped under a large oak. The Starets raised his eyes and with inspiration said, "Pray, Iosif, servant of God. The spot on which we stand is holy."

"How could it be holy?" rejoined Dikovsky. "On holidays the town youth comes here to make orgies and you call it 'holy'."

"No, no!" said the Visionary Starets with confidence. "Truly I say that here on this spot where we stand, God's grace will radiate. There will be a church built here. The oak will be hewn and this will be the place for the construction of the church altar and your entire orchard will be turned into a monastery for women by a regal wife who will be both builder and head of it."

The prediction of the Starets was precisely fulfilled.

In 1888, the wife of Grand Duke Nikolai Nikolaevich, Grand Duchess Alexandra Petrovna, was living in Lipky, a suburb of Kiev. Nearby, there was a tiny monastery which she had built. She now began to search in the neighborhood of Kiev for an appropriate place to build an entire cloister. Feodosiya Ponyrkina, a daughter of Dikovsky, heard of her intentions and suggested to the Grand Duchess that she acquire the piece of land belonging to Dikovsky for this purpose. Her Imperial Highness sent her deacon's wife to Dikovsky, ordering her to look over this orchard and to bring back a plan of the land. She was very pleased with the plan. Dikovsky's orchard was acquired and soon, through devout zeal and the Grand Duchess' means, the Pokrovsky Monastery for women was built.

When the Grand Duchess heard of the prophecy of Starets Feofil, the regal nun was completely amazed. "My God! Is it really true?" she exclaimed. "Why wasn't I told of this earlier?"

"It completely escaped my mind, Your Highness," replied Ponyrkina.

The Grand Duchess immediately sent a nun to the Kitayevskaya Hermitage with the order to have a panikhida sung at the grave of Starets Feofil. From then on she devoutly honoured the memory of the Blessed One, even ordering a portrait of him painted for herself.

KIEVO-PECHERSKAYA LAVRA

III

*"Lo, then would I wander far off and remain
in the wilderness"* (Psalm 55:7).

On 1 December, 1844, because of his age and weakening
strength, Hieroschemamonk Feofil requested a transfer from the
Kievo-Bratsky Monastery to the Kievo-Pecherskaya Lavra and
to be appointed to the Bolnichny Monastery. Instead of this,
Metropolitan Filaret assigned him to the Goloseyevskaya Hermitage near Kiev and he was given the cell of the late Hierodeacon Evstafy. For some reason or other, the service record
of Starets Feofil was not transferred with him and so, until his
death, he was not enumerated in the Kievo-Pecherskaya Lavra.

Winter passed, spring and summer came. As talk about the
Ascetic grew, it attracted large numbers of zealous people to
the charming location of Goloseyevskaya Hermitage. **A city set
on a hill cannot be hid,** said the Saviour (Matt. 5:14). It is even
impossible to hide a sweet-smelling flower in wild grass for
it will be found by its perfume and scent. In the same way
the Blessed Feofil could not be concealed in the solitude of his
hermitage. The fragrance of his holy life began to spread far and
all those who sought spiritual advice and comfort became aware
of this fragrance. And all those who came to Kiev to worship
in its holy places also went to the Goloseyevskaya Hermitage in
order to see and to talk with the Starets. But the Blessed One
greatly increased his foolishness in order to avoid worldly glory
and constant contact with people.

When Feofil entered the Lavra, the monastery's superior paid
little attention to his "oddity." According to the lists of recom-
mendations from the superior of the hermitage, Igumen Grigory,
he is mentioned in 1845 as being "capable and careful in obedience, honest, meek, and humble in behaviour;" for 1846, "little
capable, disrespectful, self-concerned, and self-willed." In 1847
he is described by Hieroschemamonk Moisey as being "little capable; he goes to church; he lives peacefully and quietly." But
in 1848, when controversy arose over the strange behaviour of
the Starets, he is recorded as "not capable for anything at all;
he is without any obedience, is stubborn and arbitrary; he is
fifty-nine years old."

In order to examine these references to Feofil and similar
references from the Goloseyevskaya superiors, Metropolitan Filaret gave an oral order to the superior of the hermitage, Hiero-

schemamonk Kallist, "to test the capabilities of Feofil." As a consequence, a report was filed on 20 October, 1848, that Hieroschemamonk Feofil "performed the whole week of services and

Church in the Goloscyevskaya Hermitage.

in our judgment cannot correctly and ceremoniously conduct a religious service." The Metropolitan agreed with this and he forbade the Blessed One to take part in services and only allowed him to communicate the Holy Mysteries in his priestly vestments on Saturdays "for the saving of his soul."

A prophet is always without honour in his own land. After this decree, Feofil was removed from the hermitage and was transferred to the so-called Novopasyechny Orchard. The Starets enjoyed it there very much but it was an extraordinarily long way to walk to church. In spite of this, the Blessed Feofil never missed a single service and always appeared at God's temple before the ringing of the bells. He had been known from his youth for his zeal for church services.

"O Lord, I love the splendour of Your house and the place of Your glory. Only grant, O Lord, that I may live in the house of the Lord all the days of my life, to see the beauty of the Lord and to visit His holy temple."

On entering the church, he usually prostrated himself three times in the centre of it. Then crossing himself at the icon before the ambo, he stood for a while either there or went over to the south door. If the women surrounded him there, he would go away to the western door and make signs of the cross in the air, as if driving someone away through the power of the cross.

"Where did all of you gather from, dark powers? God will

arise and His enemies will be scattered," the Starets would say aloud, irrately.

Then, before the beginning of the hexapsalmos, he would enter the kliros and begin reading the psalms. The actual reader, considering Feofil an unwanted accomplice, would try to stop him but, having received a rebuff from the Blessed One, he would present the book to the Starets. The Blessed One read with great inspiration but in an extraordinarily toneless voice. The singers who were dissatisfied with his reading would remark to him:

"Read more loudly, Father. Nothing can be heard."

But the Starets, to the contrary, would lower his voice and read even more quietly. After finishing the third psalm, he would hurriedly close the book and remove himself from the kliros to the centre of the church, leaving both the reader and the people in great bewilderment.

Sometimes the Blessed One would rush into the church during the Great Doxology or at the end of the service, at the time of the singing of "Under Thy Mercy" or, if the service was a liturgy, during the "Cherubic Hymn" and, pushing the people aside, he would kneel in front, raising his arms upwards with his gaze towards heaven, praying loudly. Then he would quickly leave the church, followed by a crowd of worshippers attracted by him.

It is said that the Blessed One's power of prayer on those suffering afflictions and illness was unusual. By its action many of the ill and crippled were healed. An official, Maria Grigorievna N., was possessed with fits of raving. When she turned to the Blessed One for help, the Starets read the Gospel over her, then firmly hit the woman on the head with it. As she fell back from the pain, he loudly pronounced:

"In the name of our Lord, Jesus Christ, I command you to leave!" and immediately the woman was healed.

"If you want to be well," the Starets said as he blessed her, "live at the Kitayevskaya Hermitage and do not venture out from there." Maria Grigorievna lived near the Kitayevskaya Hermitage until her death and daily attended church there.

One of the Metropolitan's singer's, Nikolai K---lov, had such overwhelming passions of the flesh that he was considered possessed since they did not leave his mind day or night. One day in spring, while taking a stroll in the woods, he met Starets

Feofil. Hoping to avoid any conversation which might lead to a discussion of his affliction, he tried to turn aside.

"Haloo, Nikolai, wait up," the Blessed One called out to him. "Where are you going? Come here to me. We will delight in lascivious thoughts together."

K—lov felt that he had been accused and wept sorrowfully before the Starets.

"Well, that's nothing. The Lord is merciful," the Starets said to him in consolation. "Let's go and pray to Him."

He knelt and began to pray. In half an hour he rose and, with a tender face, turned to the sufferer saying:

"Well, go. Lascivious thoughts will no longer disturb you."

Immediately after this the youth was healed of his ailment and his body was no longer consumed with lascivious passions.

The Blessed Feofil lived for more than half a year in the Novopasyechny Orchard but on 29 April, 1849, by an oral decree of Metropolitan Filaret, he was transferred to the Kitayevskaya Hermitage near Kiev.

Here Starets Feofil increased his podvig of foolishness-for-Christ's-sake. Although he found a new cross to bear in the form of various trials and persecutions from the superiors, he also received the consolation of solitude. The Kitayevskaya Hermitage was surrounded by high hills covered with thick woods. The Starets used to go deep into them, and there, in God-contemplating solitude, he poured out his soul in prayers to Him Whose **eyes are ten thousand times as bright as the sun and shine upon all of man's doings and see into his most secret places** (Sirach 23:27, 28).

He often went and knelt upon the stump of a large hewn tree for whole days, endlessly bewailing the corruption of the times and praying for the forgiveness of the sinful world, blind to what it is doing.

Feofil was occupied constantly and exclusively with thoughts of God and with prayer and paid no attention whatever to his appearance. He was concerned with the beauty of the soul, not with the cleanliness of the body. His clothes were threadbare with many patches sewn on with white thread and spotted with dough and oil. Even when going to church, the Blessed One put his mantle over his shirt and with cowl widely spread, he walked along the street bare chested. On his feet he wore torn slippers or else a worn out high boot on one and a felt boot or a bast shoe on the other. His head was sometimes tied with an old, dirty towel.

Many mockers would notice the old bandage on the Starets' head and ask him with laughter:

"Father Feofil! What ails you today?"

"Are you a doctor?" the Blessed One would sternly reply and walk away from them.

Another time, to the contrary, he wished to appear too healthy and thereby expose the corpulent gluttons. He placed a down-pillow on his stomach and walked about the yard. Then he walked through the monastery gates towards the woods where he met some postulants chatting idly and he reproachfully shook his head at them:

"Why were the scribes and pharisees judged?"

But the cheerful young people had noticed the large artificial stomach on Feofil and replied with peals of uncontrolable laughter.

But even this untidiness, constantly seen and reproached by all, had a distinctive significance for Feofil. It was noticed that the more slovenly he was dressed, the more his spirit struggled, the more strengthened and ardent were his prayers and the more thoughtful his forehead became.

The Blessed One always prayed in secret. Before beginning his cell rules, he donned his mantle and when he read the Gospel and the akathist, he would light three votive lamps in memory of the three times he was saved from the water. He wore a metal belt with an icon of the Epiphany fixed permanently onto it. So that he would not be idle for a moment the Blessed One spun wool, knitted socks and wove sackcloth which he usually gave to icon-painters for their work. During his work he would recite the Psalter which he knew from memory and other prayers. Each day he made countless prostrations before the icons and gave his weary body very little rest. For this he either leaned back against the wall or lay on the stove-bed across which he placed a log or sat in the middle of the cell on a short, extremely narrow bench so that if he should lose himself in sleep, he would fall off and awaken, quickly returning to his prayers.

Nevertheless, the superior of the hermitage, Hieroschemamonk Iov, detested the Blessed One for his podvig of foolishness and constantly observed his living and behaviour. He could never find the Blessed One at prayer and soul-saving exercises. No matter when he visited the Starets in his cell, the Visionary always knew he was coming. Removing his outer garments, he would topple over onto his bench and feign sleep. In this way he followed the word of the Lord Himself, Who said:

"But when you pray, go into your most private room, and closing the door, pray to your Father in secret; and your Father Who sees in secret will reward you in the open" (Matt. 6:6).

By means of his secret, prayerful works and podvigs, he was building an eternal house in heaven and laying up the provisions which are for eternity.

The Blessed Starets' cell was always unkempt, jammed and covered with layers of rubbish. When asked why he permitted his cell to be that way, he answered:

"So that everything surrounding me will constantly remind me of the disorder of my soul."

Some elders of the Lavra had visited the cell of this man of God and they related that it was filled with rows of pots and crocks containing prepared foodstuff for visitors — groats, tea, oil, flour, sugar, bread, tarts, honey, roe, fruit, fish, grapes, tapers, and such.

Understandably, his collection of provisions aroused some envy in the monastery, particularly amongst the younger members. These youths wanted to get into the food and worked out one especially elaborate plan. Having noticed that the superior of the hermitage detested Feofil, they convinced his favourite sacristan, Polykarp, to petition Iov in favour of transferring the Starets to another cell. Polykarp was quite willing to do this since he hated the Blessed One as much as did the superior. It seems that Feofil had a habit of gathering up a whole pile of worms, beetles, cockroaches, and bugs into mattress ticking and then releasing them all in church where they would crawl away into every corner. Alas, Polykarp was then required to search for this crawling army and sweep all of its soldiers out the door. In a fit of anger, Polykarp would fall on the Blessed One with abuse and often beat him but the Starets would only stop before him, fold his hands and keep silent.

"The crafty one has destructive thoughts," said the Prophet Isaiah. **"He contemplates bonds in order to ruin the poor man with words of falseness, even if the poor man is right."** That was the source of Polykarp's hatred for Feofil. Having cast aspersions on the Blessed One before the superior, he would receive an order from him to move the "guilty one" to another cell. Polykarp then would go immediately to the Starets with a malicious smirk.

"Father Feofil! The superior has ordered you to move to another cell."

"**Direct my steps according to Thy word,**" the Starets would humbly reply. And taking his mantle under his arm, an icon, and a Psalter, he would quickly go over to the cell indicated to him. And the postulants would just be waiting for this. Under the pretext of carrying over the "furniture" (the Blessed One had nothing in his cell but a lectern, a bench, and a crude table), they would get at the provisions. But Starets Feofil would not in the slightest be disturbed by the loss of the delicacies and, in the gentleness of his angelic heart, he would exclaim:

"**Wondrous are Thy works, O Lord!**"

IV

In order to avoid similar occurrences and also to help eradicate evil which had arisen in people, the Blessed One began to accept cell-mates to live with him. They did not come from among the brothers but rather, he selected them directly from the laity. The Starets paid no attention to the selected person's behaviour, whether it was vicious or not, so long as he was possessed of a keen heart and an open soul and hoped for correction.

Once, a ragged wanderer called Ivan came to the Kitayevskaya Hermitage. He was a deserter from the military service who had committed a whole series of crimes since he had deserted several years earlier. The Starets met him in the monastery kitchen and, having revealed his secret sins, brought the heart of the wanderer to repentance. Seeing this extraordinary monk before him, Ivan was amazed and would not leave the side of the Starets. He began tearfully to repent of his crimes.

Yes, there is great need for me to repent. I committed much evil on earth," Ivan concluded and sighed heavily.

Starets Feofil looked him over from head to toe, shook his head with pity and also sighed deeply.

"Do you know the parable of the talents?" he asked him.

"I know nothing, Batiushka. I was born a fool and I shall die a fool," Ivan replied with contrition.

The Starets told him of the parable of the talents and, having explained the contents, continued:

"And so our life is a time of investing. One must be quick to use it in order to acquire all that is possible. If you brought bast sandals to the bazaar and, instead of sitting with your arms folded, contrived to call buyers in, then, having sold everything, you can buy whatever you need for yourself."

"But, dear Batiushka, when and where am I to get these talents? I am illiterate, foolish, simple. I haven't got any."

"Not true! The Lord gave something to everyone who was born. It means that each person has something with which to invest and to make a gain."

"But where then! Where are they?"

"Well, just look at yourself carefully and you will discover what talent you have and how you can use it for gain. On that dreadful judgement day, everything will be asked about:

Did you have hands? What did you acquire with them? Did you have a head and tongue? What did you acquire with them? The reward will not be given for the fact that you acquired but for what it was that you acquired."

For a whole day after this conversation, Ivan stood aside and observed the Starets, amazed at his simplicity, humility, and wisdom. Finally, towards evening, he was inflamed with a desire to live under the spiritual direction of the Blessed One. He approached Feofil and with cries fell at his feet.

"Batiushka! Take me unto you! Don't let my soul perish in sins and vice!"

"Very well, very well!" answered the Starets. " **'Who comes unto me will never be turned away.'** I see that your heart truly desires to work for the Lord. Come and live with me and save yourself but bear in mind that since I possess nothing, you can expect to experience cold, thirst, grief, and deprivation. And do not complain about this fate when you begin to endure it."

"My true father! Even if I had to give up my life for you, for the Saviour's sake, I am prepared to do so."

From that time on Ivan began to serve the Blessed One and became his first cell-mate. Starets Feofil was strict and, with a vigilant eye, followed the development of his spiritual improvement, intercepting each wave of evil which arose.

Once, the Blessed One was brought a large piece of cured fillet of sturgeon. Tempted by the gift, Ivan appropriated it for himself and ate it. But suddenly he felt a terrible pain in his stomach and he began crying out, begging for help.

"Suffer, suffer, brother. This fish is being digested in your stomach," the Starets said jokingly to him. And then he added, "Why did you listen to the enemy? Why did you become led into partaking of food which ought not to concern you?"

But he saw the open-hearted repentance of the guilty one and pitied him. The Starets prayed a while and the illness disappeared at once.

In this way he educated his cell-mate by means of various works and foolish orders which, although strange in essence, had in them a great benefit for the development of his mental purity. Mixing his speech with spiritual directions understandable to him, the Starets very soon succeeded in cleansing Ivan's heart from everything bad, all his vices and temptations.

The grateful cell-mate acknowledged his insignificance before the Starets. Seeing his unchanging fatherly love and care,

Ivan paid the Blessed One for this with the most tender dedication and childlike obedience.

"Ivan!" the Starets said to him one day. "Take a basket and let's go gather some mushrooms."

They took what was required and set out into a very dense thicket of woods. The air was very hot. Starets Feofil gathered mushrooms but all the while he sighed:

"Ah, what a storm is approaching. What a storm!"

Ivan looked up. The sky was azure, limpid, and clear.

"There will be no storm, Batiushka. There is not a cloud to be seen."

"Oh, there will be one very soon. It's already approaching us. Here it is!"

At that very moment, three strappling young fellows with clubs lept out from bushes and angrily ran up to the Starets.

"Aha, we've caught a monk! Give us money!"

The Starets crossed himself, then peacefully rummaged in his basket and handed over the largest mushroom, saying, "Eat to your heart's content."

"What?" the robbers cried out. "You are even laughing at us?"

And they began to beat him all over.

"Ivan, go away!" the bloodied Starets whispered.

"No," replied the faithful servant. "Where the master is, his servant is also there." Seeing the blood on the Starets, he threw himself at the robbers in a frenzy. But they were twice as strong and, tying up the cell-mate, they also beat him unmercifully. Having enjoyed themselves over the defenceless sacrifices, the robbers disappeared.

Then Ivan understood what kind of a storm had been approaching them.

The Starets' second cell-mate was a retired soldier named Kornily. He was an unusually obstinate and stubborn fellow and, moreover, had a very sharp tongue. Visitors to the Blessed One suffered various insults from Kornily and often complained to Feofil about the coarseness of his cell-mate.

"You don't know how to behave as an eremite," the Starets told Kornily sternly. "I'll send you to the Lavra. There they will soon drill you, you bear."

And he sent Kornily to the Lavra's guest hostel. As a consequence, when Igumen Agapit was appointed superior of the Lavra's guest hostel, he took Kornily as his cell-mate.

Agapit was a great starets and his name was long remembered by those who benefited from his charity. He used to buy whole pieces of broadcloth, sackcloth, and other material in order to sew clothing for men and women. All this he gave to poor pilgrims. Aside from the constant distributing of money, clothing, and bread, Father Agapit also gave monthly pensions to a sizable number of truly poor and burdened families in the city. He accepted single people into the Lavra almshouse, feeding, clothing, doctoring, and admonishing them into salvation.

It was with this Starets that Kornily found himself. True, it was not easy for Father Agapit to get along with Kornily. Still, eventually he tonsured him, named him Nestor, then buried him and remembered him with love. But it is necessary to pay a tribute to Kornily. He was irreplaceable in the secret charities of Father Agapit and, in general, he was dedicated to him with his soul. Father Agapit did not limit his charities to the Lavra. He liked to visit the city prison, refuges of extreme poverty, and generally, truly poor people. On such trips Kornily used to accompany him. They would load their driver with parcels of clothing and, taking baskets of white bread and money, they set out for the city as if to make purchases at the store. Actually, they were conducting spiritual business by visiting the needy. They would clothe some, give money and bread to others. After that they would fill their baskets with some goods for the sake of appearance and return home happy and content. After his transference to the Lavra, Kornily was truly transformed from and ignorant "bear" into a worthy pupil of his great starets-teacher.

The Blessed Feofil foretold this long beforehand. When Father Agapit (Timofey Milovanov "in the world") visited the Starets for the first time in the Kitayevskaya Hermitage, he was told:

"When you will become superior of the Lavra hostel, this crank Kornily will serve you. He argues with and scolds everyone but he will get along with you."

A certain Panteleimon was the Blessed Feofil's third cellmate. After the death of the Starets, he lived at the Lavra hostel until old age. He told many of the elders of the various miracles of the Blessed One and of his wonderful forevision which he himself had witnessed many times.

Once, on the orders of his Starets, Panteleimon was carrying dinner from the refectory when he slipped and dropped the food near the threshold. In order to avoid chastisement, the confused cell-mate began to sweep up the food in the hope of refilling the dishes. But the Starets came up to him and said:

"You don't know to carry out an obedience, Panteleimon. You won't become a monk until you are dying." And so it happened. Panteleimon, who lived to a very old age, remained only a postulant until just before his death when he was tonsured a rasafor monk and given the name Feodosy.

Nevertheless, Panteleimon was absolutely obedient to his starets.

Blessed Feofil obtained permission to travel to Voronezh for the twentieth anniversary of the uncovering of the relics of Saint Mitrofan, Bishop of Voronezh. His postulant, Panteleimon, went with him on the long journey. Having arrived in Voronezh they spent their days in church and their nights in the courtyard near the belfry. When they had finished their podvig of reverence to the Saint, they set out on their return trip home. Having walked for a long way, they finally reached Kiev.

"It would be nice to make one last halt," said Blessed Feofil and sat down in the field to rest in the open air.

Having eaten a little food, he reached towards the bag to take out the water-gourd. But it was not there.

"Panteleimon, where is our tankard?" the Starets cried out in disappointment.

The cell-mate thought for a while and then remembered:

"Why it's in Voronezh, Batiushka. It was left where we ate last night, there at the foot of the belfry steps."

"How bad you are! Go back and get it before it disappears."

Panteleimon did not even pause for a second thought but set out for Voronezh, not even spending the night in his own cloister which was only half a verst from their position, as if the gourd constituted some sort of valuable rarity, or as if it were only a few steps between Kiev and Voronezh instead of a great distance.

He reached Voronezh safely and to his joy he found the gourd at the very place where it had been left. Taking it in his hands, he set out for home. The simple-hearted Panteleimon did not attach any significance to this podvig and was not conceited because of it, nor did he grumble against the Blessed One. He knew that the eremitical fathers of the East even ordered their postulants to drive oak stakes into the ground and water them daily in order to avoid idleness.

Once, during the Great Lent, when the Blessed One would not eat for days at a time and prayed to God in secret, he sent Panteleimon to the bazaar to buy some rather large tops from old boots. When the obedience was fulfilled the old boot tops were brought to the Starets who spread them out on a bench, side by side, and ordered Panteleimon to sew them together into several large sheets. Then he brought in a pot of wheel-tar and diligently began to smear these leather sheets.

"Why are you doing that, Batiushka?" Panteleimon asked with curiosity.

"God commands it; God commands it," the Starets quickly replied.

"And what does it mean?"

"It means, my dear friend that the evil ones write the works of sinful people on them. But today all this is smeared over and there are no more sins."

"By means of this action," Panteleimon later explained, "the Starets wanted to show that the sins of the spiritual children close to him, for whom he so fervently and constantly prayed in those days, were already forgiven by God and their conscience was cleansed before the face of God."

"There were times in the summer," Panteleimon related, "when the Starets would call me and say: 'Pick some fresh apples in the orchard tomorrow (and he would specify exactly how many). In the morning, at sunrise, go to the woods along the road. There you will meet a party of pilgrims. Give each one two apples.' I would carry out these orders, picking exactly the number of apples specified by the Starets. Then I would go to the appointed place and, lo and behold, I would give each pilgrim two apples and have precisely the required number. The Starets often gave me such orders and I marvelled at his forevision."

The fourth cell-mate of the Starets was a certain Kozma. He was an extraordinarily well read and religious servant, so that even Starets Feofil jokingly called him "theologian." For days at a time Kozma was occupied with the reading of the holy writings and books of the holy fathers. Moreover, he often forgot not only food and drink but even about direct obligations of his cell obedience. His absent-mindedness reached such a degree that when he once had to sign a paper on the occasion of receiving some documents, Kozma not only forgot his surname but his Christian name as well so that others had to remind him of it.

Of all the inanimate objects of this world, Kozma loved only books, and most of all, his old worn out Bible which he always carried with him on a belt. At night, he placed it under his head for a pillow. Kozma treated his starets with slavish respectfulness and was ready to rush, upon his word, into either fire or water. Of all the creatures of the earth, Kozma disliked women most. God forbid that he should happen to meet any oncoming female while going to the Dniepr for water in the morning. Kozma would then consider himself profaned for the entire day and, upon returning home, he would sprinkle himself with holy water. All of his thoughts and desires were directed towards the goal of retiring into the heart of a forest in his declining years, to dig a small cave there and move into it, beginning a soul-saving podvig.

Once, when he was contemplating such unattainable bliss and was building castles in the air, Starets Feofil came up from behind and unexpectedly asked:

"Kozma! Where will you live when I move on to that other world?"

"Where God commands," Kozma answered with amazement. "I will join some monastery."

"No, you are not going to be a person of the monastery. You will live among women in your own town."

Kozma shuddered from such an unexpected thought. This prophecy was equal to a condemnation and brought him into great confusion and anxiety.

"To live outside of the monastery and with women yet! No! Deliver me, O Lord, from such a disaster!" Kozma thought to himself.

But soon the prophetic words of the Blessed Starets came true.

A year after this conversation, Feofil died and his cell-mate Kozma left for his home town of Bogodukhov where he settled in a little hut on the outskirts. There he led a purely ascetic life and was famous in the entire district as a batiushka experienced in spiritual direction and advice. It soon happened, however, that, due to the labours of a wealthy woman and several generous donors, the land next to Kozma's place was bought up for the building of a public almshouse out of which grew a monastery for women.

Kozma was not a witness to the final growth of this cloister, since he soon became ill and passed away, having lived for a long time as a neighbor of the original sisters of the almshouse. He had lived, thus, "with women," as it were.

After Kozma's death, his land was given over to the newly built cloister and the memory of this remarkable starets is even now reverently remembered.

V

Blessed Feofil's stove burned both winter and summer or, more correctly, it smoked away. He would place a thick, unsplit log into it and then have to relight it several times. It is understandable that from such heating in the cell, especially in winter, it could not be warm and the water in his cell often froze. But Starets Feofil did not pay any attention to it. He would put on his sheepskin coat and felt boots and turn to his prayers. His spirit was carried high above all the needs and wants of his emaciated body.

Once in summer, when the Starets was in the Kitayevskaya Hermitage and lived in a small wooden shed, the superior sent some stove-makers to repair the ancient stove in his cell. But Feofil bribed the stovemakers not to touch the stove. The superior, Hieroschemamonk Iov, was so outraged that he took the stove-damper away from the Starets with his own hands, and moved him into a stone building in order to watch him more closely. The Blessed One, not forsaking his podvig of foolishness, hired his own workmen and ordered them to break up his stove in order to rebuild it according to his own whims. His plans were intercepted, however, and put to a stop. In September of that year, at the conclusion of vespers, disregarding the absolute forbidding of the superior, the Starets decided to light his stove.

Having put earthenware pots on the stove, he went off into the woods, leaving the stove unattended. In his absence, the fire fell out onto the wooden floor which began to burn with much smoke. The monks ran in and, with difficulty, extinguished the fire. The culprit of this disaster was not quickly found but when he returned he began to comfort everyone.

"Don't grieve about what there wasn't; it is better to praise the Lord for His mercy, for He does wondrous works for His earthly sons," he said.

The Starets received his food from the monks' refectory and he usually mixed it into one dish disregarding that there might be both bitter and sweet in it — both borshch and kasha, horse-radish and kvas.

"It is the same in life," he would say to anyone who was amazed by his strangeness, "both bitter and sour and salty mixed with sweet and all this must be digested."

The food which he prepared for strangers or the poor, he left in the same condition as when he received it from the refectory. For himself he sometimes prepared dumplings, semo-lina porridge or noodle soup. But he used neither salt nor oil and thus it all had an extremely repulsive taste.

In general, Feofil used very little food. On Wednesday and Friday he ate nothing at all except for half a small cup of honey mixed with cold water and ice. This also composed his food on Saturday and Sunday of the first week of the Great Lent and on Saturday of the Holy Week. On the other days of Holy Week, he did not even partake of water. The Starets did not use tea and instead he used to boil mint and would prepare up to two cups, but he always drank only half of each cup, pour-ing the rest into earthenware pots to treat strangers. The Blessed One did not eat the rich black bread but used only white or rush, and then he avoided the crust, pinching out bits from the centre.

But in addition to all these strange habits, the Blessed One had another original feature; love and sympathy for birds and animals.

There was a small square of land which ran from the fence of the Kitayevskaya Hermitage right up to the edge of the monastery pond. Seeing that the land was not being used, Feofil hired a peasant to plough up the land and seed it with hemp.

"Why do you need hemp, Batiushka?"

"Because the heavenly birds will come here and eat it."

The peasant did as he was told. The hemp grew and whole flocks of birds flew there to feed and nest.

Once a large number of mice invaded the Starets' cell because of the various provisions found in it. Feofil, exas-perated by their nightly raids, decided to put an end to them. He called in a young reader and said, "Catch me the superior. Catch him and I'll give you money for a sweet bun."

"How can he be caught when he always sits in his cell? Go ahead and try it. He'll take a stick to you and you won't forget it as long as you live," the reader answered with a smile. He thought Feofil was talking about the superior, Hieroschema-monk Iov.

"No! Not that superior, you silly fellow."

"Well, which one, Batiushka?"

"One who catches mice. Catch an unfortunate tramp of a cat. He will be industrious in his work. A household cat will only put on airs and sleep on the stove-bed."

Soon a tom-cat was installed and the mice were suppressed.

But now, alas, cockroaches and beetles began to pester him. Then the Blessed One called his cell-mate and said:
"Here, take this money and buy me a little hen."

The cell-mate went out and, instead of a little hen, he brought a little rooster. The young rooster would walk about the cell, shaking his red comb, picking up insects in every corner. But towards morning, when the tired Starets would doze off after a night of prayerful podvigs, it would suddenly cry, "'Cock-a-doodle-doo!"

"'This is not monastery life," the Starets decided. "Take it away from here! Take it away!" he said to Ivan, his cell-mate.

"Where shall I take him?" the cell-mate asked, only half awake.

"Take it to the postulant, Nikifor. Give it to him from me."

The cell-mate obeyed without question and took the rooster to Nikifor.

Before entering the monastery, Nikifor had been a serf and served as a lackey for his master. Being inclined towards a religious life, he asked the master to release him. Then he came to Kiev and entered into the brotherhood at the Kitayevskaya Hermitage. He had been living there for three years but unclean thoughts were confusing him and driving him from the monastery.

Having received the rooster, Nikifor stood and thought, "Why did the Starets send a rooster? I don't eat meat, but people will see this rooster and convict me of it anyway." But because of his humility, he accepted the rooster into his cell.

The rooster being disposed of, Feofil now acquired a little hen. After about a month, the postulant Nikifor came to the Starets for advice. The Blessed One said not a word but gave him the little hen.

"For goodness sake! What is this for, Batiushka? I have more than enough with the rooster."

"Take it; take it, I tell you. This gives you a pair."

Several days later, Nikifor met a beautiful girl by accident and was carried away with passion for her. He secretly slipped away from the monastery and soon married her. Only then did he understand what the rooster signified and why he was given the hen for "a pair".

It was a great distance to the Lavra and the city and so the Starets had little chance to go there. As a result, the Blessed

One acquired a bullock with which to ride to the Lavra and the Bratsky Monastery.

How he happened to acquire the little bull is an incident worth relating.

Ivan Katkov (the butcher from Podol who had brought the horse to Feofil at the Bratsky Monastery) came to the Starets for confession and while telling the Blessed One about his affairs, he mentioned that he acquired a young bull of a very unstable nature.

"I bought a bullock, Batiushka. I had planned to keep it myself but I don't know what to do with it. The brute has become stupid and gores at everyone with its horns. I suppose I shall have to butcher it, sorry as I am about it."

"Then give it to me," said the Starets.

"To you? God have mercy, why it's impossible even to approach him! Several people have already been crippled by him."

"Never mind. We will teach him humility."

"But how can I..."

"Very simple. Go up to him and say, 'Look here, little bull! From now on you are no longer mine, but Father Feofil's. Prepare to visit him'."

The butcher did exactly as he was told. Upon returning home, he walked up to the bullock and repeated the words of the Starets, and the bullock, who had been snorting and pawing the ground, became as meek as a lamb. It began to quietly caress and lick the man's hands. Then a worker slipped a rope over his horns and by dusk the young bull had been settled with Father Feofil at the Kitayevskaya Hermitage.

Now that he had the little bull, the Blessed One built a small cart with a little sailcoth hood set up on hoops in the rear of it. The Starets would travel to the city in this contraption. He never sat in front of the cart, but always in the rear with his back to the bull. He had placed a small analoy under this hood and he would fall on his knees and read his beloved Psalter as he journeyed. But here is what was so astonishing. The bullock had neither harness nor reins, but only a yoke. The bull went precisely where its master wanted to go without any command, directions, guiding or prodding whatsoever, whether it was to Podol, the Lavra or the Bratsky Monastery. It is said that the bullock even went around stones, ruts, and ditches in order not to jog the Blessed One from his reading.

But we should not be at all astonished that this unreasoning creature obeyed him thus without a whip, that a formerly fierce animal became as tame and meek as a sheep before him. Wild animals have only become fierce because of the cruelty of human nature. Remember the state of our forbears in paradise. All living creatures saw the light of the image of God in their faces and even the most ferocious animals, sensing the wondrous fragrance of this image, peacefully bowed their heads before **Adam.** When man ceased his obedience to God's commandments, God's image in him darkened. The unreasoning creatures stopped recognizing and obeying him. The fragrance of God's image was exchanged for the stench of passions and man himself became similar to the unthinking beasts. His disobedience to God was punished by the disobedience to him of the earth's creatures and man himself now fears beasts which were once submissive to him. But God's holy ones, through obedience to God's commandments, restored the image of God in themselves and, taking unto themselves the gifts of the Lord's Grace, radiated the original purity and light. Therefore, the animals, again sensing in man the fragrance of original purity, become obedient to him. What power there is in love and virtue!

In the city everyone knew the Starets. No sooner would he appear on one of the main streets than merchants would begin to run from their shops shouting, "Feofil is coming! Feofil is coming!" And each one hurried to drop something into his cart; one a piece of calico, a second a loaf, a third a handkerchief or a skein of threads. It was noticed that anyone who tried to give the Starets something from his own goods, without fail made good profits in his business that day. The Starets kept nothing of this for himself. All that was in his cart he passed out to poor people whom he met on the way. There were many of them and they would run behind the Blessed One in great crowds.

Many stories are recorded of the odd events which took place on these trips. For example, being aware of Metropolitan Filaret's dislike for him, Feofil tried even more to annoy the venerable Archpastor with his foolishness. Once in summer, when Vladika was spending some time in a cottage in Goloseyevo, Feofil arrived in his cart and drove straight into the Metropolitan's garden. The gardener was amazed.

"God be with you Father Feofil! Where are you going?"

The Blessed One paid no attention to him and instead turned back towards the way he had come, only this time he travelled down a path lined with grapes on either side and so narrow that one hardly could even walk down it. The route lay right below the very window at which Metropolitan Filaret was standing. Vladika was furious. He dashed out onto the porch.

"What is this disgrace? Who dared to let Feofil into the garden? Why did he come here? Send him away immediately. He will ruin my grapes."

The Blessed One, who had gone up the alley almost to its end, met Vladika face to face and, hearing the Archpastor's anger, calmly turned his bullock around.

"If it is not pleasing, then it is not necessary."

And, instead of leaving the garden by a wider path, he turned and travelled back down the same alley, between the grape vines.

"It is a wonder," the terrified gardener later related, "that the Starets was able to travel between the grape bushes, but it is an even greater wonder how he contrived to turn the cart around in such a narrow space where it was hardly possible for a man to even walk through. A miracle! Truly a miracle!"

From that time on Feofil fell into disgrace. The bullock was taken away from him and sent to the pastures of the Lavra. The Blessed One was forbidden to appear at the Goloseyevskaya Hermitage, or to roam around. But on the day the bullock was placed in the monastery herd, such an unusual loss of cattle took place that the Lavra steward lost all self-control and absolutely did not know what to do. Veterinary doctors were called, and it was thought that some sort of epidemic had broken out in the herd. The doctors examined the cattle and could find nothing wrong with them. Meanwhile, the livestock continued to fall and die. It was decided to report the situation to Metropolitan Filaret. Vladika summoned the Lavra steward and asked to know exactly what day the loss of cattle began. The steward replied that it was from the very day when Feofil's bullock was taken from him and put in with the herd.

"Is that so!" Vladika cried out and ordered that the bullock be quickly removed from the herd. When this was done, to the general amazement of everyone, the loss of cattle ended at once. The bullock was led away to Kitayev and returned to his owner. Having received back his pet, the Blessed One gilded his horns and peacefully resumed his daily travels.

In truth, **the ox knows its owner** (Is. 1:3).

The road from Goloseyevo to Kitayev used to be unbelievably narrow. At the beginning of the Kitayev woods, the road rose up a steep hill. At this point, a narrow ravine crossed the road and it was necessary for travellers to descend into the ravine to cross it. It happened once that Metropolitan Filaret and Archimandrite Lavrenty, the Deputy Superior of the Lavra, were hurrying along this road to conduct business at the Kitayevskaya Hermitage. Just as Vladika's carriage reached the middle of the ravine, Father Feofil appeared with his "steed". The Metropolitan's coachman thought that this was an approaching peasant and he sternly cried out:

"Hey you! Turn back! Turn back, I tell you!"

The Metropolitan, on hearing these stern calls of the coachman, thrust his head out the window and asked, "What is it?"

But, upon seeing Feofil approaching towards him, he at once guessed what it was.

"Ivan, stop!"

The coachman stopped the horses, and Vladika and the deputy superior stepped out of the carriage. Feofil was sitting in the cart, leaning his elbows on its rail, and pretending to be asleep.

"Feofil, get up! Misfortune has occurred!" Metropolitan Filaret said loudly and began to awaken the Blessed One.

"What? Ah! Is it you, holy Vladika?"

"It is. Why are you dozing, you mischievous person? Just take a look at the trouble you have caused us."

And the trouble was great. The meeting occurred at the narrowest place and it was impossible to turn around either the bullock or the carriage.

"Well, what will we do now?"

"We will do something," Feofil answered peacefully.

There was nothing to do but to unhitch the bullock. Vladika drove him back up the hill with a stick while the Deputy Superior and Feofil pulled the cart after him. The coachman did not participate in this "podvig" since he was holding the horses. After several efforts the road was freed and the Archpastor could finally continue his journey. Vladika was in good spirits and upon bidding farewell to Feofil, he laughed loudly.

"Just see, you mischievous person, how much sweat you

have rolled out of us," wiping large drops of perspiration from his forehead.

Soon after this the road was widened, but only slightly, and travellers still ran into difficulty in the ravine. Again the Blessed One and Metropolitan Filaret arrived at that very spot at the same moment. Although this time Feofil could have turned around, he refused to do so. It was as if he premeditatedly blocked the Metropolitan's way. An argument erupted between the coachman and Feofil. Father Feofil argued that it would be more difficult for his one bullock to draw his burden back up the hill than it would for Vladika's four horses to return up with theirs. But the coachman stood his ground.

"Feofil is right," said Vladika, observing the scene. "We should have made way for him. But since it is not possible for a team of four horses to turn around here, be kind enough to turn around with your bullock, Feofil."

But the Blessed One remained stubborn and did not wish to fulfil the request. The Archpastor began to become agitated.

"Well, what about it? Will you stop trying my patience?"

"No, I won't stop, because it is you and not I who must turn back."

"How so?"

"Just so."

At that very moment, a dispatch rider rode up to Vladika with a message from the Lavra. An artisan had fallen from the scaffolding around the belfry of the St. Sophia Cathedral and had been killed.

"He had hung in the air for a long time, holding on to a rail, but did not hold out and fell to the ground," the messenger said, and asked Vladika, in the name of the Lavra Superior, for immediate instructions.

The shaken Archpastor did not say a word in reply, but crossed himself and ordered the coachman to go to the top of the hill to turn around and return to the Lavra. Feofil was no longer there. At the arrival of the dispatch rider he drew back, having finished his mission.

They met again for a third time. On this occasion the Blessed One was returning to Kitayev from the city when the Metropolitan's carriage overtook him and drew up alongside him on the Dyemiyev Bridge. Vladika called out:

"Feofil! Where are you off to?"

"Wherever God leads and necessity calls. Only there is

trouble. The bullock has stopped listening to me. I have ordered a long whip to make him obey."

"And why do you want to ride with him at such a tortoise's pace?"

"The way to the Kingdom of Heaven is slow and steady."

"Here, climb into my carriage and I'll get you there as fast as a falcon."

"Thank you, I don't wish to. I will get there before you all the same."

Just as Feofil had foretold it, so it happened. Because of the overly fast pace of the carriage, a wheel slipped off Vladika's carriage and it required a whole hour to repair it. When the Metropolitan arrived at Kitayev, Feofil met him at the gate and, bowing low, he said:

"I wish you health, holy Vladika. I have been waiting for you here for a long time."

"You are right, Feofil," replied the Metropolitan. "The horned bullock overtook my well-fed team. It would seem that in the future I will have to travel in such a manner."

Many people remember this bullock which usually was not tied, but roamed freely around in the Starets' yard. It is said that the bullock possessed an almost supernatural instinct and could guess, without error, the character of the people who came to the Starets for his blessing. For that reason, he met some visitors in an unfriendly and bellicose manner, while others were treated gently, allowing them to pass unhindered into the Starets' cell.

Aside from his love and compassion for animals and birds, Starets Feofil had other customs and habits. To begin with, he disliked smokers and could not bear the smell of tobacco.

"You see, you've become intoxicated with the devil's poison," he would sternly reproach his visitors who smoked. "You've come to the cloister to spread the tobacco infection. Of what good is it for you to approach the Holy Mysteries tomorrow with that tobacco on your breath? Go away from me! You don't have my blessings!"

Once Feofil was walking along a lane of the monastery yard with a devotee from the city and was carrying a crock of grated winter-radish in kvas, when he was approached by Viktor Ignatievich Askochensky, the editor-publisher of the journal "Domestic Discussions". He was puffing away on a cigar. As he opened his mouth to speak, he exhaled tobacco smoke right into Feofil's food. The Blessed One said nothing but dipped his finger into the crock and sprinkled the smoker with some of the liquid.

Upon returning home, Askochensky sat down to dinner, but the dish served had an overwhelming odour of winter-radish. Askochensky did not suspect the cause of this. He only sent the serving back and asked for another. It was brought, but again, the same odour prevailed. At this point Askochensky became angry and began chastising the cook and servants. But there was no explanation for the odour. The second course was served, and again, the dish set before Askochensky reeked of winter-radish. It was the same with the third course. Askochensky became very agitated. He stormed out of the house and went to the home of a friend. Upon being received by his friend, he was greeted with the comment that he smelled strongly of winter-radish. Nevertheless, he asked his friend for something to eat, explaining about the careless preparation of the food at home which rendered it inedible. How great was his amazement when even at his friend's table the food reeked with the odour of winter-radish. Utterly bewildered, he went to the bakery to buy some cookies. He returned home and sat down to tea and cookies, but, alas, they too bore the stench of winter-radish. For three days poor Askochensky was driven to utter despair. Everyone he met commented on how much he reeked of winter-radish.

The unfortunate man tried desperately to find the cause of this phenomenon and finally he remembered the encounter with Starets Feofil. Conscious of the impropriety of his act, he set out to Kitayev to the Blessed One. He begged forgiveness and straightway the unpleasant odour disappeared.

Another incident is related by a nun, Staritsa Magdalina.

"Once, a wealthy merchant and his wife arrived from Moscow and stopped over at the Florovsky Monastery. Having heard our stories about Starets Feofil, the merchant became excited with a desire to visit him. He begged me to accompany him and his wife since he was not familiar with the way to the Kitayevskaya Hermitage. I agreed and we all set out. While riding through the Goloseyevo woods, the merchant desired to smoke. He felt his pockets, but there were no matches. What was he to do?

As luck would have it, he saw some wayfarers sitting beside the road making porridge in a trivit. He went over to them and began to light his cigarette. But no sooner had he touched the fire than the trivit turned over, spilling out the porridge and smothering the fire.

'How strange! I didn't even touch the trivit and yet I upset the porridge.'

We went on farther. The merchant again spotted some strangers cooking gruel by the side of the road. He ran to their fire for a light, but just as he stooped towards the fire, this trivit also upset.

'What a strange occurrence! Could this be some sort of witchcraft?' the merchant laughed.

'No,' I said to him, 'Father Feofil is arranging this for you. He dislikes with a passion those who smoke.'

At last we arrived at Kitayev and went to see Starets Feofil. He met us and spoke out directly to the merchant.

'Well, my little swallow, you wanted to smoke so badly? Due to your passion, you left the hungry without food.'

Then Feofil brought him a large onion from his cell, saying:

'Here, take a bite of onion, for you have befouled the entire monastery with tobacco'."

This was the kind of visionary he was.

Another rule which was peculiar to Starets Feofil was that he never spat on the ground and advised others not to do so either. He was particularly indignant with those who spat in God's temple on the floor of the church.

"Why do you spit in church?" he used to ask all those who did it. "God is invisibly present here and people kneel to Him in prayer. And why do you spit on the ground? Don't you know that you yourself are earth and ashes, so how can you dare to spit on your own mother? Is it not she who will take you into her bosom after death? Is it not she who will guard your body until the general resurrection?"

VI

Few people had the chance to approach Starets Feofil for his blessing. He spent entire days in the woods at prayer and would return home to the hermitage only towards vespers in order to be in time for the beginning of the Divine Service. If anyone succeeded in approaching him, the Starets would give his blessing without stopping, as if in a great hurry. In general, the Blessed One disliked having attention turned upon him and thus being distracted from his prayers.

When he noticed pilgrims waiting for him on the road, he would turn off somewhere to the side, into the bushes, or if it was in the cloister itself, he would climb to the top of a large oak growing near the hostel, or he would hide in the monastery orchard in a deep hole which he had dug for that purpose.

The keeper of the orchard was a "learned gardener", Ioakim Panfilych, one of the Lavra postulants, a master of his own work and well-liked by Metropolitan Filaret. He would become very irritated with the Blessed One for hiding in the orchard while his admirers trampled through the garden searching for him. Several times Panfilych scolded the Starets and finally, irritated by his constant gentleness, the gardener struck Feofil in the face. The Blessed One was not confused by this and, as if answering with gratitude, bowed to the ground before the offender.

"Judge, O Lord, those who offend me, struggle with those who struggle with me," he whispered quietly and added, "Ioakim, do not dream that the Metropolitan likes you. You will never be a monk."

Soon the words of the Blessed One were proven true. Ioakim was transferred to the Lavra Caves and from there he was soon removed completely from the monastery because of some of his actions.

Feofil particularly disliked meeting with intellectuals and those who rose above the ranks of the common people. Most of all he disliked the so-called "coach people", that is, those who came in coaches, often for the sole purpose of looking at Feofil as some sort of oddity.

"What do you want of a smelly creature like me?" he used to ask his persistent admirers. "What are you seeking from me, a wretched, poor starets and a great sinner?"

"A kind word, Batiushka, advice, instruction, comfort," the visitor usually replied.

"Go to Schemamonk Parfeny. He will teach you, but I have nothing to say. Turn to the All-Holy Theotokos and the holy fathers of the Pecherskaya Lavra with pure faith and they will give you all that is necessary, but I have nothing."

Moreover, the Starets sometimes pushed away those who stood near, and quickly walked away from them. And in reality, what answers could he give them? They usually asked purely worldly questions. Some would ask for his advice for the successful outcome of their lawsuit in which a poor man would have to suffer, others tried to find out if their son would receive a prominent position with an eminent person; another wanted advice on marrying a son to a wealthy bride, or a daughter to a famous groom. Some even asked for prayers to receive great rewards or high pensions. But few even thought to get advice on the one thing that is necessary for man — the salvation of his soul.

In order to avoid similar useless receptions, and to escape from undesired, tiresome visitors, the Blessed One selected a very original means. He would spread tar or pitch on the doorstep of his cell and would thus be delivered from idle talkers.

But if a truly pious and simple person, thirsting for a useful word should appear, the Starets willingly accepted him, although not spending too much time with him. Feofil would absolve him with a stern reproach which revealed his secret sins.

"It was strange to see," witnesses have said, "how the Blessed One heard the confessions of the people who came to him. He did not ask for their sins as spiritual fathers usually do, but having placed his saintly hands on the head of the person confessing and looking up to heaven, he himself listed all the secret and known sins. At this, not only did the penitent shed tears of emotion, but from fear and shame, even the hair of his head would stand up on end."

In the town of Vasilkovo, there lived a profiteer who had made a fortune in shady business dealings. All his life had been lived in depravity, dishonesty, and evil. He had built up a large estate for his old age, but having retired to take advantage of it, he became afflicted with a gnawing conscience. He resolved to repent of his sins and seek forgiveness. He had heard many stories about the great podvizhnik, Hieroschemamonk

Feofil, and he set out for Kiev in the hope of spending some time with him.

The visionary Starets, foreseeing the visit of the profiteer, decided to anticipate his arrival by meeting him before he reached the hermitage. For this purpose he set out into the woods and for days awaited the merchant on the road where the Red Tavern was located. Soon the carriage appeared with the profiteer-merchant seated importantly within. He noticed the monk walking in his direction, and he came out of the carriage and walked towards the monk.

"How do you do, Batiushka!"

"Well, and how do you do, sir merchant!"

"Is it far from here to the hermitage?"

"Which one do you want?"

"Kitayevskaya."

"It is high unto God, far to the Tsar, but the hermitage is closest of all. What is your matter? To pray to God?"

"Something like that, but most of all I want to see the schemamonk that is called Feofil. You couldn't tell me where he lives?"

"Of what use is he to you?"

"They say that he is very holy, a visionary."

"Who, Feofil?"

"Yes, the hieroschemamonk."

"What kind of holiness is that? You have believed all that old wives' nonsense?"

"How could this be? All say..."

"You don't say! But he is such an evil-doer, such a fornicator, you couldn't find such a villain in the whole world. He ravished other women, seduced maidens, stole his neighbors' horses at night, lent money to the poor at outrageous interest rates. How many orphans he has let out into the world without any clothing, how many people he has destroyed through shady business and deception! He has grown a fat belly on other people's goods and now he has the desire to approach God. He has come to Starets Feofil with a pile of deathly sins on stolen horses. Well, repent, repent. Pray to God. The Lord is merciful. He doesn't want a sinner's death, only his change to a life for Him."

But the amazed horse-dealer had already felt in his heart that this was Feofil and had already dropped to the feet of the Starets, weeping tears of repentance on them.

"Forgive me, Batiushka. Absolve me, accursed murderous swindler and villain that I am."

"God will forgive, God will forgive. Go to God's saints. Bow to them. Pray to them. They will expiate you. They will forgive everything. Your father was a righteous man and for his prayers God will have mercy on you."

"No, He will not have mercy on me. I have angered His infinite benevolence too much."

"He will forgive, He will forgive. Only don't fall into errors again through carelessness and thereby litter the beneficent sources which have cleaned the soul today by your repentance. Don't cease praying, don't give freedom to your passions. Guard your forgiveness, love and retain the fear of God. Go!"

The merchant promptly set out for the Lavra and spent many hours telling the monks of the caves about his encounter with Feofil.

On another occasion the Blessed One met a passing landowner in the Kitayev woods and said:

"Where are you going?"

"Home, Batiushka!"

"And have you settled up with God?"

The landowner was puzzled but went ahead without a reply.

"You didn't settle?" said the Starets following him. "So remember, you came here well, but you will not return home healthy."

And what happened? On the return trip, right next to the town gates, the horses bolted and overturned the carriage. The landowner fell against a stone and was killed.

And here is another case.

Near the city of Kerch on the Taman there lived a colonel's widow named Alexandra Sokolova. She and her sister went to Kitayev and she asked the Starets for his blessing.

"Teach her, the silly thing," the Blessed One said to the sister, pointing at Sokolova. "Teach her better, or else she will ride horses until her death."

But Sokolova gave the words no significance. Upon returning home to her estate, she ordered a carriage to be harnessed and set out for Kerch on business. The horses became frightened of something on the road, bolted and Sokolova flew out of the carriage. She died that very day.

And there was another incident. Once Starets Feofil came to the Great Lavra Church and having found a place for himself at one of the stalls along the walls of the church, he began to pray. During the reading of the Kathisma, he decided to go and reverence the tombs of the saints reposing in the church

*Cathedral of the Dormition
in the Kievo-Pecherskaya Lavra*

and he left his Psalter at the stall and went to the tomb of Saint Feodosy. The reader and the assistant regulator noticed this and decided to play a joke on Feofil by hiding his Psalter. The Blessed One returned to the body of the church and he did not even glance at his former standing place. Instead, he walked straight to the assistant regulator who had hidden the Psalter in his pocket.

"Oh elder, elder. You must die tomorrow and you want to play evil tricks today. Woe unto you."

The prediction occurred precisely. On the next morning, the elderly monk suddenly died.

Starets Feofil maintained a good supply of clothing in his cell as many philanthropic persons would send him all manner of garments for his charities. The Blessed One would spot a tattered person and immediately invite him to his place and feed him dumplings and give him a new shirt or even re-clothe him from head to toe.

Once a worker from the Lavra brick factory, Ivan Bolshakov, came to him. He had received his monthly wages but went straight out and drank it up to the last penny. And so, ragged to the utmost, he went to the Blessed One for charity.

"Why alms for you?" the Starets asked him. "You'll drink it all just the same. But here, let me give you a new shirt. You will die today and it will not be becoming to lie in the coffin with rags on."

Ivan Bolshakov received the new shirt and thought, "Just you wait for me to die. I'll dash over to the tavern right now, sell the shirt and have a good drink to your health."

He did just as he had planned. He drank himself into a stupor and towards evening he came to the brick factory. He danced, sang songs, and played the fool. To all those present, he related how he got the shirt from Feofil and about the death prediction. Finally, he asked permission to sleep at the factory and having received it, he climbed up into the highest berth, right under the ceiling. During the night there was a sudden loud thud. The lights were put on and there was Ivan Bolshakov lying on the floor, his face all blood, not breathing. They felt his heart but there was no beat. The poor fellow was dead.

What was to be done? Bolshakov did not even have a shirt to be buried in, so the workers used anything they could find to put on him. He was given a Christian burial but the story of the shirt and the Starets' prediction are still talked about.

A noblewoman, Maria Kozminishna Shepeleva, often came to the Kitayevskaya Hermitage with her four year old son, and she always went to Starets Feofil for a blessing. The Blessed One liked her very much and each time he met her in the monastery yard he would look at her young son and say, "Aha! Here comes a little monk."

Once he called the child to his cell and gave him a pile of treacle-cakes. "Hold out your hands. Eat the cakes." The boy ate them up with gusto and the Starets encouraged him, "Eat, eat. When you grow up you will accept Christ, not treacle-cakes."

The Starets' prophecy came to pass. The child grew up, was sent to the Lavra printing shop for instruction, then he became postulant and later a spiritual father in the Lavra, respected by all.

Once the Blessed One called to his cell-mate, Pantelelmon, and said:

"Bow to the feet of this boy. Kiss the hand of your spiritual father."

When the boy grew up and became a hieroschemamonk, he tonsured Panteleimon before the latter's death and then buried him.

The chief supervisor in the building of the Kiev-Vladimir Cathedral, Kondrat Kozmich Khovalkin, wishing to spend the remainder of his days in peace and tranquility, began to build a house for himself in Kiev but grief suddenly befell him. His favourite daughter died, the single comfort and consolation of his lonely life. With sorrow in his heart, Khovalkin set out to Starets Feofil for consolation.

"Why do you grieve?" the Blessed One answered him. "Sit in a cell and say the prayer of Jesus, 'O Lord, Jesus Christ, Son of God, have mercy on me, a sinner.' Everything will pass."

"It can hardly pass, Batiushka. In the face of the deceased one the light of my life perished for me."

"The light of your life is the unsetting Sun, Jesus Christ. Buy yourself a mantle. You will soon be a monk."

Sometime later Kondrat Kozmich entered the brotherhood of the Goloseyevskaya Hermitage as a postulant, built a monastery hostel there, and began a podvig of salvation. Soon he became blind, was tonsured into monkhood with the name of Erazm and lived for several years in solitude in a small cell near the church. When he died on 15 August, 1880, he was buried several steps from the grave of the starets, Parfeny.

A middle class youth of Kiev, Ferapont Dobrovolsky, felt a great desire to become a postulant at the Lavra. For three days he went with his mother to see the Starets for a blessing, but Feofil kept avoiding talks with the visitor, sending him either to the hostel or to church. On the third day when Ferapont and his mother became fairly hungry and it seemed that their visit would have to be prolonged, the youth turned to the cell-mate Ivan for help. He took pity on them and sent Ferapont to the Starets' cell.

"Why are you hanging around here, grovelling? Am I a saint?" the Starets angrily asked the youth.

In a minute he sent out a little piece of bread and soaked cabbage for Ferapont and his mother. The instant the young man tasted the food. he felt his hunger had disappeared. In half an hour the Starets again came out of his cell and Ferapont, seeing him, fell at his feet.

"Give me your blessing for the Lavra, Batiushka!"

"What kind of blessing shall I give you? You will never become a priest-monk. Go to the Lavra and live the life of a common monk. Only live well. Don't eat fish on Wednesdays or Fridays and don't ever miss the matins service."

Ferapont Dobrovolsky was accepted into the Lavra and was tonsured a monk with the name Spiridon. For fifty-one years he lived in the Lavra as a plain monk, faithfully fulfilling the directions of the Blessed One, never missing even one matins service.

A navigator from the city of Kerch, Andrei Gapchenko, came with his wife, daughter and a sister, on a pilgrimage to Kiev in 1851. The pilgrims spent several days in Kiev and having seen the places of interest, they set out to Kitayev to see Starets Feofil.

The Blessed One came out to them from his cell and turned directly to Gapchenko's wife, Evdokiya Trifonova, asking her:

"You live near the sea?"

"Yes, near the sea, Batiushka."

"And is your estuary deep?"

"I don't know, Batiushka, I didn't measure it," Evdokiya Trifonova answered in amazement, glancing frightenedly at her relatives.

"On Wednesday and Friday buy incense and candles and give them to the Church for the salvation of your soul, for you have taken to business and sell only fish."

With these words he blessed everyone and left.

The pilgrims left and stopped for a while at Pochaev to pray, then once again came to Kiev and having left their daughter in the Florovsky Monastery in the care of the nun Angelina, they set out for Kerch alone.

Some time passed. On 28 June, on the eve of the feast day of the Holy Apostles Peter and Paul, Andrei Gapchenko had to leave home on a very urgent business matter. But he fell very ill and had to send his wife in his place while he remained at home in Mitrodat. Evdokiya Trifonovna set out on the trip with her one year old daughter, Paraskeva. It was necessary to cross over the estuary by boat, but the ferries were full, so the young woman had to embark on a launch loaded with lime.

Soon the launch opened its sails and sailed out into the open sea. That night there was a sudden desperate cry:

"Save yourselves — we're sinking!!"

It happened that a large leak had opened up on the bottom of the launch and the vessel began to sink to the bottom. In terror, many threw themselves into the sea, others jumped into life boats, still others left themselves to the mercy of fate. Evdokiya Trifonova did not lose her presence of mind and with fervent prayers she turned to God for help. Half an hour passed. The vessel was sinking deeper and deeper. And now the deck was covered with water and Evdokiya stood in water up to her knees — implacable death came closer and closer.

"Bless, O Lord!"

With these words, Evdokiya crossed herself, tied her child to her back and courageously began to swim. With desperation the young woman struggled with the water, with ten-fold strength her arms cut through the swift waves of the deep sea and all around was darkness, continuous water. Nowhere was help to be seen. Her hands began to numb and Evdokiya strained herself to the utmost. Having turned on her back, she moved her child over to her bosom and, holding it with her teeth, she swam farther and farther, not knowing where. And the shore was far off; very far.

She seemed to see her family waiting for her return with terror.

"Farewell, my dear ones! Farewell!"

Her strength weakened and her arms could no longer move. She felt that she was slipping somewhere into coldness, into the depths and a terrifying darkness was covering her eyes.

Andrei, overcome with grief, searched for a long time for his drowned wife and God pitied him. On the third day the waves washed her corpse ashore near Taman with the imprint of terror on her face. The ill-fated companion of his life lay silently on the shore holding in her numb arms her little dead daughter pressed firmly against her maternal breast.

Having buried his deceased wife near that place where she was washed ashore, Andrei Gapchenko set out for the Kievo-Pecherskaya Lavra and there he was tonsured a monk with the name of Malachy. He died at the age of eighty-two.

When leaving home, Blessed Feofil never locked his cell, not even when his cell-mate was also away, for, even in his absence, there was aways a group of people, mostly women, near his cell. There was no getting rid of them. They would come to him even before going to church. They would run after him in a crowd, having waited for him for a long time at his window.

The Starets often received people clad only in his coarsely spun under robe, regardless of their rank. When he opened his door, the women vied with each other in trying to bring him some gift. One would shove a pitcher of milk, another cheese or eggs, a bottle of kvas, and so on. And dear God! What a desperate business would take place. Each one tried to give her goods into his hands. Each one wanted some attention turned to her.

In thankfulness for what was brought to him, Starets Feofil provided them with a variety of chores to do. Some brought water, others wood, or he would send some to dig in the garden or white-wash a stone. Among them were also pompous ladies. The Blessed One did not stand upon ceremony with such. He made them carry out the slops and garbage, mix dough or peel potatoes.

A married noblewoman once came to Feofil. There was a great crowd in front of the Starets' cell, so she pushed and shoved her way through. She began to call out:

"Batiushka. your blessing! Batiushka, your blessing!"

"And you came to me for a blessing?"

"To you, Batiushka, to you. I wish to speak with you."

"Very well, right now."

The Starets went into his cell and brought out a large bowl of cabbage soup.

"Hold up your hem. God will bless."

And he poured the cabbage soup into the upraised skirt. The woman was horrified. She had on a new silk dress. But the Blessed One did not give her a chance to speak and interrupted her angry thoughts.

"You are unfaithful to your husband daily. And who came to ask me for a blessing in a silk dress? I'll give you what-for, seducing young people with beauty. I'll give you what-for!"

Another time an important landowner came to the Blessed One. Surrounded by a whole suite of manor serfs, she stopped in her carriage in front of the residence of the Blessed One and, with a smile, began to look about in all directions through a lorgnette.

"Tell me please. Where does Feofil live here?" she haughtily asked the cell-mate who came out to her.

"There he is digging in the garden."

The curious lady glanced back and, seeing the Blessed One digging beds while wearing nothing but his under robe, she spat aside with contempt.

"Fie! What ignorance! Walking about the monastery in nothing but a long shirt!"

"In nothing but a long shirt," the Starets said, mimicking her as he came up closer. "Eh, you white-handed princess! And why have you stripped your serfs to their last shirt? And why did you let them out into the world without a piece of bread? To ruin people there is no conscience, and yet, before a humble monk shame appeared? Repent, excessive pride! Love your nearest ones or else it will be bitter for you when your sinful soul will stand in the nakedness of shameless matters before the face of God's judgment."

This outpouring so stunned the woman that she immediately leapt out of the carriage with tears of repentance and spent a whole hour in the Starets' cell, begging him for forgiveness and prayers.

And there were others. There appeared, one day, a very punctilious noblewoman. The Starets was not in the cloister at the time the admirer arrived to receive a blessing. As usual, he was out roaming in the woods. But some people who were at the top of the Kitayevskaya belfry saw the Starets returning home. He was walking with his head lowered and had dirty rags and towels hanging from him. God only knows where he got them! One of these towels was soiled beyond belief with excrement. Walking up to the noblewoman, Feofil stopped and said in a plain Little-Russian dialect:

"Oh, this is a great lady! My hands must be wiped."

And he wiped them with the soiled towel.

"Here, kiss it!" he said stretching out his hand to her.

She, you can understand, stepped back in horror.

"And such are your virtues before the Lord God," the Blessed One said sternly. "They stink, my lady, they stink!"

Even the eminent philanthropist and devout Countess Anna Alexeevna Orlova-Chesmenskaya was not spared by the Starets. The Countess once came to the Blessed One on the advice of Metropolitan Filaret. When she asked for his blessing for the beginning of some important matter, the Starets did not answer a word, but gathered up a pile of fine sweepings and poured it into the skirt of her dress. Orlova was so devout and honoured the Starets so much that she left, humbly carrying the sweepings, and all the way home she contemplated about the significance of this action of the Blessed One.

Another time she came to him on the eve of the Feast of the Dormition. The Starets was in the habit of cleaning up his cell on this day. He was washing pots and dishes when Countess Orlova arrived. Seeing her, he exclaimed joyously:

"Ah, a maiden, a maiden has come! Opportunely, very opportunely. Pray, dear one, go down to the Dniepr and wash a couple of little pots for me."

He handed her an armload of dirty dishes.

Anna Alexeevna only smiled and, without any embarrassment, went down to the Dniepr where she diligently took to washing the pots, dirtied with age, with her own hands which were decorated with precious rings. Her servant stood at a respectful distance and marvelled, seeing the Countess at such menial work.

The Starets did not speak openly with everyone. With many he explained himself through parables filled with significance. Moreover, he had the custom of giving the visitor some thing, not significant in itself, but prophetically hinting at the fate awaiting him. A crock, a sliver of wood, a rotten apple, a pear, a piece of pie, a cucumber, a rag, a prosphora, a candle nub, even a handful of manure which was often found in his basket. For the Starets all this had a symbolic significance relating to a specific person.

Once he sent his cell-mate to Hieromonk Modest, the regulator of the Lavra, with some dirty foot-cloths.

"Give them to him and let him wash them," the Blessed One said to his cell-mate.

After a while the foot-cloths returned clean.

"Aha! Not so!" the Starets exclaimed. "Take them again. Let him wash them whiter."

And he sent them off to Modest for a second time. What did these dirty foot-cloths signify? They signified unclean thoughts which were confusing the regulator at that time and they were sent to him to be washed until the monk's mind was cleaned and received a flow of cleaner thoughts.

Hierodeacon Agapit, who subsequently became igumen, was appointed recorder of the Great Lavra Church. This obedience, being very troublesome and active, was not in keeping with the personality of the hierodeacon. He had to have constant conversations with the many pilgrims who visited the Lavra. He was expected to entertain guests and satisfy the curiosity of all visitors. All this reduced his contemplation and studying time to a minimum. Despondency once fell upon the devout Agapit, and when this happened, a messenger from Father Feofil suddenly appeared with a prosphora with the instruction to eat it, at which his despondency disappeared.

Once the poor widow of a psalm-reader came to the Starets. She wept before him, complaining about fate. Her relatives refused to help her even though her family was large and almost dying from hunger.

The Starets looked at her attentively and with his own hand he wiped the tears rolling down the face of the widow. He then went into his cell and brought out a large bowl of cabbage soup.

"Here you are. Pray, take comfort. But once you have received, see that you don't give away to anyone. They didn't help you, now don't you give to them."

"But I haven't anything to give away, Batiushka."

"Well, well, see that you don't give. Hide everything for yourself."

The widow returned home with the cabbage soup. As soon as she arrived in the village, she received the news that a childless cousin had died and left her a large estate. Her greedy relatives who had ignored her poverty now took note of her wealth, but she gave them nothing.

Another time a peasant came to the Blessed One with his daughter.

"Why did you come?"

"Batiushka, bless my daughter to go away to a monastery. She is so good, kind, and obedient. Her mother and I long ago promised to dedicate her to God. Bless her."

"Good, yes, I'll bless her right now," said the Starets and disappeared into his cell.

The peasant waited to find out what would happen next. The Starets brought out a tallow candle and removed the wick from it.

"Here you are."

"What is this for, Batiushka?"

"It is your daughter's blessing. Now begone!"

Half a year later the "good, kind, and obedient" daughter

gave birth to a child. There was no more talk of virginity or a monastery, only of a wedding.

Two peasants of Saratov province, Iona Kirillov and Demian N. set out for Holy Mount Athos. On the way there, they stopped in Kiev to pay their respects at the revered places and to visit Starets Feofil for his blessings on their journey.

"You cannot go to Athos. Stay here," the Starets replied to them. "They won't permit you to go."

The young men did not listen to him and went to Odessa. The Russian ministry would not grant them exit visas however, because of the mounting tensions with Turkey.

The friends returned to Kiev and were accepted at the Lavra as postulants. In a week's time they visited the Blessed One. Starets Feofil brought forth a three-kopeck bun and, dividing it in half, gave each one an equal sized piece.

Soon the friends were separated. Demian was sent to the Sarov cloister while Iona remained to live in the Kievo-Pecherskaya Lavra.

Maria Matfeevna Genzo, the widow of a wealthy landowner of Kherson, had been involved in a court action concerning land with her brothers-in-law for several years. Due to her lack of astuteness, she had lost the case and now faced complete ruin. In desperation she had appealed to the Senate for a reversal of the court's decision. Having heard of the Starets from devout friends, Genzo travelled to Kiev to seek the advice of the Blessed Visionary.

The Starets was living at the Kitayevskaya Hermitage at that time and, meeting the visitor, he brought her an enormous hot loaf of white bread. This loaf was divided into two parts. In the lower half was a depression in the soft part. Into this depression the Starets had poured so much oil that it ran over and dripped onto the floor.

"Here, here, take it. Don't be bashful. This is for you from me because of your great patience."

Genzo was confused but she took the loaf. She returned home pondering over the strange gift. Soon the matter was solved, for she received word that the Senate had ruled in her favour. Not only was she to have her land back but her oppressors were required to make full restitution for all her losses and costs.

The happy Genzo sent fifty rubles to the Starets in gratitude. He promptly distributed the money to the needy poor.

An igumen of one of the monasteries in the Eparchy of Kiev relates this incident.

"In 1852, I completed the course of the Kursk Ecclesiastical Seminary and felt the desire to be tonsured a monk, so I went to the Kievo-Pecherskaya Lavra on a pilgrimage. I had heard that Starets Feofil did not bless everyone equally and before going to his cell, I sent a comrade to get his blessing while I

hid behind a tree to observe how the Starets would accept him. Feofil received my comrade in a friendly manner, blessed him and said some kind words to him. Approving of such a reception, I promptly came out from behind the tree and knelt, folding my hands to receive a blessing.

'Go away!' the Starets said to me. 'I'm not an archbishop blessing you. Go to an archbishop — he will bless you.'

I was overwhelmed. Tears choked me and I could hardly stand on my feet. My comrade noticed my condition, took me by the arm and led me from the hermitage. I don't even know how I walked to the Lavra. I only remember that my comrade was comforting me, explaining Feofil's poor reception as a happy event. I seemed to realize that this had not been an offence but some sort of test which had to be endured without a murmur and therefore I strongly relied on the intercession of the Heavenly Queen. On our return to the Lavra, we went to the Great Church, prayed there and reverenced the holy relics. Then we went out. At one entrance we saw a carriage standing with several pilgrims clustered around it. 'For whom are they waiting?' 'For Vladika. He's coming out right now.' Truly, in about five minutes the Metropolitan came out and I hurried to walk up to him for a blessing. Having explained the aim of my arrival, I expressed my desire to remain in the monastery forever. Great was my astonishment and joy when I received, at that very moment, a blessing from the Starets Vladika and he consented to my entering the Lavra brotherhood. Soon I was tonsured a monk and only then did the words of Starets Feofil become clear to me."

A peasant came to Kiev to worship and appealed to the Blessed One for advice, asking for his blessing to enter a monastery. Starets Feofil listened to him and then asked:

"Do you want to eat?"

The peasant nodded his head affirmatively.

"Here you are, eat."

And he gave the youth some soup. At the bottom of the bowl was something very hard which he could not chew. The Starets was very curious to know if the young man could manage with the object at the bottom of the soup, and he watched him through the door of his cell. But certain that the podvig was beyond the young man's power, he went out to him and said:

"Well now, that is enough. Enough. Go to Holy Mikhailovsky Monastery and live there."

The youth entered the monastery and was notable for his meekness, simpleness and mental capabilities and was even appointed assistant to the cellarer. But soon a great misfortune occurred. The cellarer, Hieromonk Mikhail (of the Orlov priests) was strongly indignant with his humble assistant and sought to drive him out of the monastery. With tears in his eyes, the postulant gathered his belongings and left them in someone's care, then hurried to Starets Feofil for advice. While walking up to the Starets' door, he began to pray:

"With the prayers of our holy fathers, O Lord, Jesus Christ our God, have mercy on us."

But the Starets did not allow him to finish. Opening his door, he sternly berated the unhappy postulant.

"You, Pavel, why have you come? Go home right now! Ah, you, Pavel! You Mikailovsky monk! Go home!"

The youth was totally bewildered, but set his feet towards the Mikhailovsky Monastery, thinking as he went:

"Well to be sure! They say that he is a visionary and he called me Pavel. What kind of Pavel am I when I'm not Pavel at all?"

It happened that the Vicarial Bishop in Kiev, Apollinary, was a very simple and just person wno took a special interest in each monk and every postulant in his see. Vladika had heard of the injustice which had befallen the young postulant and he called Hieromonk Mikhail to himself and severely commanded him to search for the mistreated one and restore him. Messengers were sent out in all directions but before they had time to find him, the postulant returned from Feofil. Vladika was notified and the innocent youth was soon tonsured and, to his amazement, given the name prophesied by Feofil — Pavel.

Maria Dudareva, the wife of a broker, had wanted to go to Kiev for a long time. Because of the cholera epidemic of 1853, she postponed the trip. She had a fanatic concern for her health. Finally, she ventured to set out. While at the Kitayevskaya Hermitage, she decided to see Starets Feofil. As she approached his door, Feofil came out to meet her, carrying a small box with a lid.

"Hello, hello, oh wife of a broker! Here, I have prepared a little box for you. Do you like it?"

"Oh yes, Batiushka, very much."

"And if we close the lid thus — will that be all right then?"

"Why, yes, of course, Batiushka."

"Well then, here take it. But beware. Go home quickly. Do you hear? Do not stop anywhere in the city or it will be very bad."

"But I came on a pilgrimage to Kiev, Batiushka. I would like to stay for a couple of days."

"Don't even dare to think about that. Go as quickly as you can."

Maria left for home immediately and arrived in fear. But she barely had time to greet her family when she was seized by writhing and retching and had to lie down on a bed. Her face turned blue and she suffered from her cholera for only three hours; then, she yielded up her soul to God.

Here is a no less interesting case. In the city of Tula there lived two wanderers, Katrina S. and her brother Ivan. They were without family or relations. Each spring they would set out for the holy places, he to the north and she to the south. With the coming of the cold, they would return home for the winter.

Thus one year Katrina came to Kiev and, as usual, stopped to see Starets Feofil. The Blessed One gave her his blessing and handed her a little clay pot tied up with paper as a souvenir.

"Here, take it. But make sure that you don't untie it before you get home."

Katrina left but on the way her curiosity began to work on her. "What could be in the pot? Probably the Starets foresaw something nice for me and put butter into the pot." Finally, she could no longer contain herself and she decided to open it in spite of the Starets' admonition not to. She untied the paper and peered into the little pot. Much to her shock, there lay a dead sparrow.

"Oh, what kind of a joker are you? Why just see what that old man has thought up. A dead sparrow," she thought.

In anger she spat and then smashed the pot against a tree.

About a month later Katrina returned home from the pilgrimage.

"What, my dear brother hasn't been home yet?"

"No, not yet," the neighbors replied, "but there is a packet here with your name on it."

It turned out to be nothing less than news that her brother had been robbed and killed on the road. Katrina then understood the significance of the dead sparrow and she broke down into bitter tears.

In Kiev there once lived a very wealthy and landed cattle dealer, A. D---ov. His wife was meek and God-fearing but D---ov himself was a coarse, cruel, and little-believing man. The wife was a regular visitor to God's temple and monasteries, liked to give alms, to receive the poor and wanderers and was very dedicated to ascetics. She was absolutely devoted to Starets Feofil and often invited him to their home. D---ov, on the other hand, was hard-hearted and dissipated and could not bear the presence of Starets Feofil in his home. He would constantly mock his wife for inviting him.

"Aren't you ashamed to spend so much time with this bigoted fool?" he asked her.

One fine morning when D---ov was not at home, Starets Feofil arrived equipped with pieces of coal. He began to draw ciphers on the wallpaper, some in tens, others in hundreds of thousands. D---ova did not dare to stop him and stood off to the side, staring in amazement at the Blessed One's activities. Her husband soon returned. He noticed Feofil's bullock standing in the yard and decided to make fun of the Starets, but when he entered the room and looked at the wall, he was horrified. The expensive wallpaper was black with ciphers written in coal.

"Who dared to do such a thing? Feofil, of course!"

And he went through the rooms to search for Feofil. Seeing him in his bedroom, he threw himself on the Starets with reproaches and swearing. But Feofil, pretending to be a fool, began silently to remove his clothing. D---ov spat, and stormed out of the house. The distraught wife, regaining her composure, began to apologize to Feofil and offered him some soaked cabbage, of which he was very fond. Instead of accepting, he gave her a stern and ambiguous answer:

"No — all is finished! God is just. I was offended, ruined, and left as a beggar. **The Lord hath given and the Lord taketh away.**"

And he immediately set out for home.

Shortly after this, the D---ov family was beset by terrible grief. Their business began to diminish, their capital began to melt away, huge depts appeared. Soon their property was auctioned off and the haughty, rich D---ov became a beggar, dragging out his existence in some wretched hovel allotted to him by the Kiev city administration out of pity and compassion.

VII

The high respect and esteem in which Feofil was held by his admirers was bound to arouse some covetousness and jealousy.

Hieroschemamonk Iov, the superior of the hermitage, was especially embittered against the Starets. Having decided that all the Blessed One did was the result of bigotry and superstition, he proceeded to cause him all the difficulty and annoyance he possibly could. The superior made Vladika weary with his constant reports and complaints. When he would see a crowd of worshippers surrounding Feofil, he would hurry outside and reproach them for their superstition and drive them away. When that did not help matters, the superior would order the monastery gates to be locked after dinner so that the curious crowd could not go up to Feofil's cell. Iov even went so far as to rush into the Blessed One's cell to take away his linen so that it would not be given to laundry women. To all this harassment the Starets would meekly make a reply from the Gospels. Often Feofil would have his cell-mate, Panteleimon, bolt the door when he knew Iov was coming to harass him.

Finally, Iov, in order to glory in his power and demonstrate his authority, moved the Starets to the bottom of a large building, nearer to himself. The new accommodation was very comfortable, consisting of four large rooms. Nevertheless, the new living place was very unsatisfactory to the Starets because it interfered with the work which God had called him to.

When the Lavra sent Hierodeacon Feodosy Tupitsin to the hermitage because he was mentally ill and required special attention, he was placed in the same cell with the Blessed Feofil. But the Starets promptly drove him away. Irritated by this act of self-will, the superior, Iov, personally led Feodosy back to the cell of the Blessed One.

"Father Feodosy! With a saint you will be a saint, with a chosen one, you will be chosen."

But Feofil ran out of the back room and again drove Feodosy away. Turning to the superior he shouted:

"Do you know how to read and write?"

"If I didn't know," Iov smirked, "I would not have become a superior."

"And you've read the books of the Bible? Well?"

"Not only read them, but memorized many of them."

"Then tell me, for what reason did Cain kill his brother Abel? Tell me, for what reason?"

And with that he led Iov out of the door and slammed it behind him. Outraged to the depths of his soul, the superior promptly reported all this to Metropolitan Filaret and asked that Feofil be sent away from the hermitage.

From all the complaints about the Blessed One which appear in the archives of the Kievo-Pecherskaya Lavra, it is easy to see how little understood Feofil was by those close to him. But he who does not know his own soul could hardly understand the soul of his brother. **For when the world with all its earthly wisdom failed to know God...** (I Cor. 1:21) then one could hardly expect the world to recognize a true servant of the Lord. But pride, vanity, and jealousy blinded many eyes to the fact that Feofil was a great servant of the Lord, chosen from his mother's womb to be a lamp of the faith.

It is not so amazing, then, that the world lies in evil. It refuses to see in the piety of these ascetics truly active sons of God. Instead, the world despises and hates those who have given themselves to praying for the world. We are surrounded with inexhaustible sorrows, uncountable troubles, and endless grief. The enemy struggles constantly against us. Yet, those who struggle hardest against the enemy and seek to save man from the wrath of God are universally condemned, despised, and persecuted. Never the less, these ascetics patiently remember the words of the Gospel, **If you were of the world, the world would love its own, but because you are not of the world the world hates you** (John 15:19).

So even his fellow monk, the superior, Iov, failed to recognize Feofil and instead persecuted him out of jealousy. Finally realizing that abuse and pejorative would accomplish nothing, Iov conceived a new idea for ridding himself of the Blessed One. He began to gather various slanders against him, hoping to have the Starets at least removed from the hermitage.

As the Scripture warns, the oppressor says, **"Let us lie in wait for the virtuous man, since he annoys us and opposes our way of life... Before us he stands, a reproof to our way of thinking, the very sight of him weighs our spirit down; his way of life is not like other men's, the paths he treads are unfamiliar. In his opinion we are counterfeit..."** (Wis. 2, 12-16).

We do not know if Iov recognized that the slanders he gathered against the Blessed One were false or not, but from his reports one thing is evident. He wanted to give these slanders the appearance of truth and so he interpreted the life of the Starets to suit his own ends. He wrote to Metropolitan Filaret that Hieroschemamonk Feofil "abuses monasticism and, through his carelessness of rank, he completely separates himself from it. He spreads superstition and bigotry. In concealing the inner part of his life with insolence and even violence, he gives rise to doubts about the state of his religious beliefs and his mental health." Was it not in this very same way that false witnesses were gathered against Jesus Christ? But the souls of the righteous are in God's hands. As hard as his enemies strove against Feofil, they could never achieve their goals.

The Blessed One was not grieved by this vain slandering. To the contrary, he rejoiced, recalling the words of the Scripture: **It is a blessing for you when they insult you for bearing the name of Christ, because it means that you have the Spirit of glory, the Spirit of God resting on you...On their part He is blasphemed, but on your part He is glorified** (1 Peter, 4:14)...**Happy are you when people abuse you and persecute you and speak all kinds of evil against you on My account. Rejoice and be glad for your reward will be great in heaven; this is how they persecuted the prophets before you** (Matt. 5:11-12).

When the cell-mate, Ivan, came to him, moved with compassion for the Starets, and asked how he could face such sorrow with seeming indifference, the Blessed One replied:

"Ah, Ivan, Ivan. It is better to endure injustice than to commit it oneself."

"And what if these things are endured in vain, for nothing, Batiushka?"

"What about it? One cannot destroy an evil person. It is sinful to give up to sadness. We are exiles on earth. Exiles do not wonder at insult and injury. We are under God's penance and a penance consists of deprivations and difficulties. We are ill in soul and body and bitter medicine is useful for the ill."

In order to quench all hostility his heart might feel towards his offenders and to fulfill in reality the directions of the Scripture: **Do not let the sun go down on your anger** (Eph. 4:26), the Blessed One would react to Iov's attacks by composing a letter confessing that he was truly guilty in the bitter incident which had taken place. Never-the-less, he increased still more his podvig of foolishness.

His manners in church, however, raised many eyebrows besides those of the superior. The Blessed One would usually turn his back on the people and face the wall, never raising his eyes. When actually serving, he acted even more strangely. We will not go into great detail about this, but only relate the words of Iov, the superior of the hermitage in his report to Metropolitan Filaret.

"While preparing for a co-service," wrote Iov, "Feofil breaks the rule and order. Before the beginning of the great vespers or matins, he ignores my confirmation and never stands in the sanctuary. No one knows where he might read his prayers. He barely participates in the entity of the liturgy or the magnificat. During the Kathisma, he leaves or stands outside the south door and during the co-service, he does not stand straight but turns to the east. Evidently Feofil never washes his hands or face. During the liturgy he stands before the altar-table as if dumbfounded and requires constant directions. He is constantly arranging his braided plait. He holds his book before himself but apparently rarely reads the required prayers and seldom does he reverence. Having wiped his nose with his hand, he bends down and wipes it with the garments of the altar-table. During the exclaiming of 'Christ is amidst us,' he fails in every way to conform to the others who are serving. Feofil partakes of the Holy Mysteries very quickly and then goes to the sacristan's door, looking at the people (as if showing off) and reads the prayers of thanksgiving. On highly solemn days, although he does participate in the service, he does not come out for any special prayers but divests and leaves the church. He has often been deprived of meals for this. During the presentation of the gifts (proskomidia) he does not place the holy bread on the centre of the paten, but on the left side which can cause it to upset easily. He does not observe the proper order in distributing the particles over the rest of the paten. During the liturgy he turns towards the analoy and does not look at the service book, apparently turning away from the holy table. He requires prompting during the entrance from the altar and during the Great Entrance at the carrying over of the Holy Gifts. He does not hold the service book before himself and does not turn his eyes and heart to the holy table while making a proper reverence. Instead he glances at the book lying on the analoy. At the moment of the sacrifice of the gifts, it is difficult to stir him into making at least three reverences and piously blessing the sacrificed gifts. Breaking the aforementioned into pieces, he

very slowly wipes the clinging crumbs from his hands with a
sponge. His tempo in the service does not conform with anyone
else. When the deacon proclaims "Fulfil the chalice, Vladika,"
he does not even look at the chalice but drops the separated part
of the Holy Lamb into it so quickly that he cannot follow proper
succession."

Metropolitan Filaret of Kiev

Metropolitan Filaret could easily believe all this because he
himself had concelebrated with Feofil and had witnessed his behaviour.

"Turn him around to his place," he would say to his archdeacon
when the Blessed One faced east while everyone else was turned
to the west. The Metropolitan could not know that there was an

enigmatic secret behind the peculiar behavior of the Starets, a secret known only to himself. He could only assume that Feofil was completely incompetent (Archives of the Kievo-Pecherskaya Lavra).

We should mention here that the most salient feature of Metropolitan Filaret's administration of the Lavra was his own humbleness. He did not rule as a powerful despot, but as a steadfast and zealous follower and a humble postulant of all the regulations and customs passed on by the monks from the saints of the caves. Both the inner and outer condition of his life served as a model to the Lavra Brotherhood. Vladika's conduct and instructions followed what "the original holy wonderworkers of the Kievo-Pecherskaya Lavra, enlightened by the Holy Spirit, established and preserved. He was, therefore, not so much like a metropolitan or a rector to the brotherhood, but like a father or elder co-brother. In a word, he was an abba, as the fathers of ancient monastic asceticism were called. His addresses, talks, directions, even his remarks and warnings were given with meekness, patience, and indulgence. He did not bring fear to anyone or distrust to himself. To the contrary, everyone ran to him with joy and frankness."

Vladika conducted himself in this manner in the controversy over Feofil. It could be seen that, while Iov's complaints were directed towards maintaining the rules and regulations of the monastery, they were composed with personal hostility for the Blessed One. The fair-minded and peace-loving Vladika called Feofil to him privately and questioned him.

"Feofil!" said the meek Archpastor to him. "Complaints about you have come to me again."

"The strong have risen against me and the mighty are seeking my soul," the Blessed One quietly answered, lowering his eyes to the ground.

"Still, what will you direct me to do with you?"

"Marvelous are Thy works, O Lord!" Feofil replied.

"They write that you are spreading superstition and tempting the brotherhood and the people."

"Deliver me from the slanders of men."

"Now then, don't go about 'delivering' but reason, brother. The superior is badgering me and asking for your punishment."

"The Lord is my Refuge and my Saviour — of whom shall I be afraid?"

"Will you tempt me?" finished Metropolitan Filaret, "I'm dismissing you, you mischievous one."

"In the Lord is my reward and my comfort is in the Most High."

With this the conversation came to an abrupt end and, having bowed to the Metropolitan, the Blessed One quickly left the chamber, leaving the venerable Archpastor in the same confusion concerning his innocence as he was in before.

As much as the saintly Filaret did not like the Blessed Starets at first, so much did he respect Starets Parfeny. Every summer he left with Parfeny for the Goloseyevskaya Hermitage, returning to the Lavra only for the feast days and then hurrying back to the hermitage as soon as they were over. There, in the most solitary corner of the hermitage, in the midst of a dense thicket of a shabby orchard, stood Parfeny's cell.

Immediately upon completing the early liturgy in the Archpastor's house-chapel, Parfeny would go into the woods, completing his prayer rule as he walked and reading the entire Psalter along the road. The compiler of the biography of Starets Parfeny, briefly but profoundly and correctly depicted his spiritual relationship with the saintly Filaret, expressing it in the following edifying words:

"Great was the love of the Saintly One for the Starets but boundless was the dedication of the Starets for the Saintly One. And this spiritual union provided comfort for both in their ascetic wandering in this life. The Archpastor's soul, often wearied by the troublesome tasks of his rank, rested in the conversation of the spiritually enlightened Starets, and the soul of the Starets leaned upon the Archpastor's wisdom with absolute trust."

Why, then, you will ask, with Vladika Filaret's monastic love and with his truly brotherly, spiritual tie with the monks of the Kievo-Pecherskaya Lavra, did he remain so cool to the Blessed Feofil, who was such a remarkable person? And why did he feel such a great love for Hieroschemamonk Parfeny, but remain almost indifferent to the ascetic Starets Feofil?

Our reply is this:

Hieroschemamonk Parfeny demonstrated a model of life similar to the great ancient ascetics, a spiritual life which shone in his face. The entire development of his spiritual perfection took place almost before the eyes of Vlaika, who, comprehending in him a truly burning zealot of holy asceticism, invested him with the schema with his own hands in the caves of Saint Antony and named him Parfeny.

Subsequently, both of these persons so tightened their spiritual bonds that the venerable Archpastor decided to select Parfeny as his spiritual father.

Hieroschemamonk Parfeny

Starets Feofil, already a hieroschemamonk and attached to the Lavra, could have reflected a high state of spiritual attainment in his countenance, but in his podvig of being a fool-for-Christ's-

sake, he concealed the irreproachable purity and child-like innocence of his soul, seeking by all means to avoid spiritual inter-
course with the saintly Metropolitan. He would not allow Vladika to see into the depths of his strange character and thus prevented
Filaret from apprehending the grace which existed within him for,
what man knows what is within another unless he comprehends
the spirit living within him?

For this reason, the disconcerted Archpastor, in his love of
justice, called a meeting of the superiors and advisers under him,
and heard testimony from others outside the Lavra, in an effort to
gather all evidence either justifying or accusing the Starets.

The matter was soon explained, for one brother, with whom
Feofil was more open with than others, approached him and asked
him about his strange behavior during church services. The Starets answered:

"I liturgize according to the correct order, read all the required
prayers, and I honour the celebrant as my leader. But when I go
deep into contemplating the fulfilment of the Mystery, I forget myself and all that is around me. During the Divine Liturgy, I see a
cross-shaped ray of light coming down from above and hovering
over the celebrant and all those serving with him. Sometimes it
hovers over everyone. I see a strange dew descending on the
Holy Gifts and shining angels soaring above the altar-table, saying
'Holy, Holy, Holy, Lord of Sabaoth; heaven and earth are full of
Thy glory!' Then my whole being is enraptured unspeakably
and I am unable to tear myself away from the sweet vision. O
brother, I am not justifying myself; I am only telling the absolute
truth. Only I beg you, do not reveal what I have said or else I, a
smelly sinner, will become a temptation to others."

Feofil's reply was immediately reported to Metropolitan Filaret. The Archpastor had already planned to transfer Feofil to the
Moshnogorsky Monastery where he would no longer be numbered
with the Lavra brotherhood. Upon hearing of this report, however, he called in the deputy of the Lavra, Archimandrite Ioann,
and the ecclesiarch of the Lavra, Hieromonk Melety, for consultation.

The ecclesiarch, Melety, had always fought in Feofil's defence,
and now he answered Vladika's question thus:

"Why disturb this righteous man? Let him enlighten us, for
no one knows who has longer to live on earth — you or he."

Vladika looked sternly at the bold adviser, and, having thought
for a while, he said:

"Yes! You are right, we are all walking under God."

And immediately he gave the order to the Ecclesiastical Sobor of the Lavra to suspend the previous restrictive orders concerning Feofil, pending further instructions.

And so the Starets remained, living in the same place as before.

On the day following the consultation, Blessed Feofil sent his cell-mate with a large watermelon to Melety. What did he foresee for the ecclesiarch? On the next Sunday, without any preliminary announcement, without awaiting permission from the Holy Synod, through his own personal authority, Metropolitan Filaret placed a mitre on Hieromonk Melety and elevated him to the rank of archimandrite.

VIII

Metropolitan Philaret was completely to reverse his view of the Blessed One. Up until this time he had doubted the holy life and forevision attributed to Feofil but his eyes were soon to be opened.

As it is well known, the prayer rule of Vladika Filaret was exceptionally lengthy and took six to seven hours to complete.

"I don't understand," he had said in his personal talks with the Lavra startsy, "how older people in general, and monks in particular, can lead their lives if they have not acquired a taste for prayer and the practice of praying. It must be unusually difficult and lonely for them. Therefore, oh how necessary it is for everyone not wishing to spend their old age in dreariness to become used to prayer early in life."

And he himself was the first to put his own advice into strict practice.

It once occurred that Vladika's presence was urgently required in Kitayev. Troubled with some heavy matters the night before, he arose half an hour later than usual and hurried through his morning routine so as not to be late for his appointment in Kitayev. While he was reading the morning prayer-rule, his cell-mate, Hieromonk Nazary, came into the chapel and reported that the carriage was already waiting at the door to take him on his journey. Vladika could not delay his departure and so had no time to complete his prayers. He called for his cassock, and quickly departed. Within half an hour the carriage had entered the Kitayev woods and Metropolitan Filaret lowered the carriage window, avidly breathing in the wonderful aroma of the fresh morning air. Suddenly his gaze stopped on a large tree standing nearby. There, at its top sat Feofil, peacefully reading a prayerbook.

"What are you doing there?" shouted the amazed Vladika.

"I am finishing the reading of my cell-rule," Feofil quietly answered from above.

"What? What did you say? Speak louder! I can't hear you!"

"I said I am finishing the reading of my cell-rule!" the Blessed One shouted at the top of his voice. "I had no time at home. The trip interfered, but at least I can finish along the way!"

"Yes, yes, yes. You are talking about me," Vladika guessed at once. "Well, thank you, you culprit, for having advised an old man like me. Come on down quickly. I will finish reading it myself."

After this incident, the Metropolitan became very interested in the Starets and began to observe him attentively. He decided to visit the Starets in his cell in order to reach a final conclusion concerning the unjust slanders brought against him. The Metropolitan would set out for Feofil's cell often, but each time Feofil tried to prevent Vladika from engaging in idle curiosity. Once the Starets even walled up to the door of his cell with brushwood and smeared it with clay so that the Metropolitan was forced to turn back.

Finally, Vladika, accompanied by his cell-mate, managed to arrive and find Feofil at home. The Blessed One received the high guest very cordially, seating him on the little bench while he went about preparing the samovar. When the water began to boil, he carried the samovar over to the centre of the room, put it on the floor and placed an earthenware bowl under the tap. Then he took the Archpastor's wooden staff and looked at it attentively from all sides.

"And what is this stick worth?" the Blessed One asked, looking at Vladika.

"It's worth nothing," replied the Metropolitan.

"No," said the Starets. "It's worth all of twenty-five rubles."

And with these words he placed the staff on the bowl which was standing under the samovar, removed the tap and threw it into the corner. The water ran out onto the staff, filled the bowl and overflowed onto the floor. Vladika stood up in great confusion, walked across the wet floor and hurried out of the cell.

Several days passed. It was June and the weather was bright and pleasant. Vladika decided to go for a walk in the woods alone. His manner of dress was such that he looked almost no different from the monks at Goloseyevo. He wore only a simple cassock and cap, carried a plain walking stick in one hand and a Gospel or Apostle in the other. He looked more like a monastery starets than a Metropolitan.

Near the end of the Goloseyevo woods there was a knoll and there, near a fence, stood a plain garden bench on which Vladika always rested. This was Vladika's favourite place because from here there was such a magnificent view; both the city and the Lavra were spread out before the eyes. Enjoying the solitude, the Metropolitan used to sit here for hours at a time, and lifting his saintly hands to heaven, he would send up his secret prayers for the well-being of those living in the holy city and the Pecherskaya Lavra.

This time he wished to perform his usual prayer and knelt
down, but just then a man with a club approached him from behind
the bushes and, pointing to his cudgel, he asked the Metropolitan:
"And what is this stick worth?"

Vladika wanted to bless him, but the stranger quickly made
his aim known:

"Don't bother, just give me what you have of value."

The Metropolitan peacefully pulled out his purse in which
there were twenty-five rubles and said, while handing it over:

"Well, brother, I'm sorry for you. There is very little here."

But when Vladika had drawn the flaps of his cassock in order
to pull out the purse, the robber had noticed a gold watch with a
chain.

"If there is so little here, then give me your watch and chain
as well."

Vladika peacefully fulfilled the demand.

"Aha!" said the stranger. "It seems to be gold."

"What of it?" Vladika began. "It would be to your advantage,
brother. . ."

"How is it that you are a monk, but you have a gold watch?
Or perhaps you are not an ordinary monk? Perhaps you are a
treasurer or something like that?"

"No, I am not a treasurer."

"Then who are you?"

"To tell the truth, I am called Metropolitan."

"Metropolitan!!" the stranger cried dumbfounded.

"Well, yes. What is it, my dear one, that makes you so
alarmed? The Lord be with you."

The stranger fell at his feet.

"Well, brother, get up and accompany me home and please
don't be afraid of anything."

As they approached the hermitage, Vladika turned to speak to
the unfortunate one:

"It would be wise, brother, if you gave me back the watch
and chain. You see, it is engraved with my name. Who knows
what trouble you may get into when you try to sell them. It
would be better if you stayed here a while. You can join us as
a wanderer and I'll even add some money."

The stranger gave back the watch and Vladika proceeded on
to the cottage. Meeting his cell-mate, Father Sergei, in the porch,
he ordered him to go quickly to the gate where he would find a
wanderer who had been kind enough to accompany him, and

invite him in. The cell-mate went beyond the gates, but the stranger had vanished.

"What an unkind person," the Metropolitan said. "Well, may the Lord be with him."

Having sat down for a while and gathered his composure somewhat, Vladika sent for Feofil and when he appeared, Filaret pointed his hand to his walking stick and said with a smile:

"Your prediction was fulfilled, Feofil. The stick is worth not less than twenty-five rubles. But that is not terrifying my friend. What is terrifying is that the malefactor could have let as much blood out of me as you had let boiling water out of the samovar."

"Wondrous are Thy works, O Lord!" the Blessed One answered with his favorite saying.

In conclusion, I will relate one more incident which finally convinced Metropolitan Filaret that Starets Feofil was not an ordinary person and that his soul was filled by the grace and gifts of the Holy Spirit.

Once, while riding through the woods in a carriage, Vladika ordered the coachman to turn off to Kitayev and, having stopped there for an hour or so, he set out for the cell of the superior of the hermitage in order to speak with him on some matters. On the way, Starets Feofil met him and instead of asking for the Metropolitan's blessings, he took a charred log from under his cassock and threw it at Vladika's feet. The other people around were astonished and thought that the Archpastor would become angered and it would turn out badly for Feofil. But the Metropolitan appeared to take no notice of the incident and continued on his way as if nothing had happened.

Soon after this, Vladika was again in Kitayev and, meeting Feofil in the monastery courtyard, stopped him and said:

"Well, mischievous one, I have not been in your cell for a long time. Today, after the liturgy, I'll drop in to your place for tea. Only see that you don't treat me with the same kind of tea as you did the last time."

"You are welcome, Your Eminence, " answered the Starets, bowing to the ground before the Archpastor.

We do not know for certain whether the Metropolitan merely wanted to talk with the Blessed One or, remembering the charred log thrown under his feet, wanted to discover from him the significance of this act, but the fact is that after leaving the church at the end of the liturgy, Vladika went directly to Feofil.

And how did the Blessed One receive him? Upon returning to his cell, he immediately ordered his cell-mate to fill a barrel with water and then add sand to it. When a fairly good "gruel" was thus obtained, the Blessed One smeared the walls of his dwelling with the mud, also the door and door-post and then he spread the mud thickly on the floor. He then covered himself with mud and sat down on the stool in the middle of the room, solemnly awaiting his high guest.

In half an hour the door to the cell opened and the Metropolitan, having stepped in, stopped near the threshold in amazement.

Mud and disorder were everywhere and the master of the cell did not look like a monk but like someone who had just climbed out of a smoke-pipe.

"What is this?" the Archpastor asked angrily.

"Have no doubts, Your Eminence. Please. It's like this after the fire. I had a fire and I kept watering and watering it and so I became dirty."

The angered Archpastor threw a scornful glance at Feofil and retreated hastily. But just before he sat down in his carriage to depart, Feofil's cellmate, Ivan, ran up to him and presented him with three bottles of water.

"From whom is this? What is it for?" the Metropolitan asked.

"From Starets Feofil, Your Eminence. He ordered me to give this present to you and tell you that it will come in handy to pour on the charred log."

"To pour on the charred log? What is all this now? And what did he pour into these bottles? Try it!"

"Water," replied the cell-mate, "plain water, holy Vladika."

"Plain water?"

"Truly it is, Your Eminence."

"Well, place it in front of the coachman. It is evident that the culprit wanted to prophesy something."

Several weeks passed during late autumn. At twelve o'clock midnight on 18-19 November, 1844, Roman Baranov, a postulant at the Lavra, lighted the stove in the prosphora bakery, and together with the other postulants, began preparing the dough for baking prosphora. The supervisor of the prosphora bakery, ryasaformonk Vasily Titov and the general supervisor of the bakery, ryasaformonk Leonid Zatvorny, were preparing to partake of the Holy Mysteries and set out for matins. Upon leaving the church, they went to their cells to read the appointed prayers.

Suddenly, at three o'clock in the morning, the watchman, a postulant of the bakery, Iosif Alferov, noticed the pungent smell of smoke while walking along the corridor dividing the prosphora bakery from the main bakery. Alferov ran to investigate the back part of the courtyard where the wood was kept and where the wooden outbuildings stood, but finding nothing amiss, he glanced through the keyhole of a door which led up a ladder into the attic and saw a raging fire. He grabbed for the key but when he opened the door, the smoke hit him in the face with such force that Alferov recoiled in fear. On closer examination, it could be seen that the wooden scaffold had caught fire near the horizontal flue which led from the stove of the prosphora bakery to the smoke stack. The brothers came running with buckets and strove to extinguish the fire, but their efforts were hampered by the inconvenience of the route to the fire and because of the arrangement of the metal roof. The fire grew stronger and stronger and soon encompassed the entire prosphora bakery. To complete the misfortune, such a strong storm was raging that night that burning wood was carried all the way to Podol and even as far as the Florovsky Monastery.

On the morning of 19 November, the fire spread still farther and penetrated under the metal roof of the Lavra printing shop. The frightened Metropolitan, seeing that the fire was increasing in size and was threatening not only the remaining buildings, but the Great Lavra Church itself, no longer hoped in the weak power of humans. He ordered the doors of the Great Church to be opened and he went there to pray. For a long time he knelt praying tearfully before the holy miraculous icon of the Dormition of the Mother of God, and he called to her in a loud voice, beseeching her help and intercession. After a while he arose, exhausted.

A sacristan had entered the church and stood at a respectful distance.

"Well, what is it?" the Metropolitan asked with a trembling voice.

"Glory be to God!" answered the sacristan. "By your holy prayers the Lavra is saved."

The Metropolitan crossed himself and sighed with relief. Then he walked out of the church and set out for the sight of the inferno. A large gathering of police, firemen, serfs, and armoury and garrison commands had been working together and the fire slowly began to die down. In several hours the flames in the printing shop and other buildings were completely extinguished.

The losses in buildings from the Lavra fire were quite insignificant since only the roofing had burned while the walls remained intact. But when the losses of the huge storage of books and printing machines were calculated, the sum was quite significant, about 80,000 rubles (Archives of the Kievo-Pecherskaya Lavra, Matter No. 2520).

After this event, Vladika became so attached in spirit to the Blessed One, that, as proof of his esteem and love, he placed Feofil together with Hieroschemamonk Parfeny and himself in the chambers of the Goloseyevskaya cottage.

"I have only the two of you. You — a schematic, Parfeny — a schematic, and I — a schematic, we shall live in the name of the All-Holy Trinity," said the Metropolitan with a fatherly tenderness, to the Blessed One while settling him into the cottage. (We may note that seventeen years before his repose in God, the Archpastor Filaret took the great angelic image, the schema, with the name of Feodosy and he guarded this secretly to the last days of his life.)

But the Blessed One had no desire to prolong this close contact, and on the first convenient occasion brought such dampness and mud into the room that he damaged the wallpaper and the painted floor, and he introduced a mass of insects into the living quarters. Not a day went by when he did not throw out some "thing." In addition, when they would all three sit down to eat, Feofil tried to spill as much as possible on the table cloth, for which purpose he would sometimes upset his dish on the table as if by accident, and thus force Vladika and Father Parfeny to leave the table early. If this was insufficient, he pretended to be ill and began to hiccough loudly and often, trying in this way to spoil Vladika's appetite. The Starets annoyed Parfeny by putting on Parfeny's boots at night, leaving only a pair of bast sandals or felt boots in their place. Then he would disappear into the woods for the entire day. Or else, in the middle of a peaceful night when all the inhabitants of the cottage were sleeping deeply, he would leap from the bed and sing at the top of his voice, "Behold the Bridegroom cometh at midnight, and the wise servant stands waiting to greet him. . . "

As if it were not enough, from the very first day of his arrival at the cottage, not regarding that it was summer, Feofil commenced heating the stove in his room, and he always did so just when Vladika was occupied with prayers or with his correspondence. Moreover, his fire let out so much pungent smoke that the cell-mates had to open doors, windows, and vents in order to air the rooms at least a little. Vladika would sit in the garden all this time in wearisome waiting.

Starets Parfeny usually conducted the early liturgy in the house-chapel of the Metropolitan's cottage, but often Feofil would appear there a quarter of an hour before his arrival and, having robed himself in his priestly vestments, he would commence the service with the sacristan. When Parfeny would arrive in church, he could only be a witness to the divine service, but could not participate in it. And Feofil, fool-for-Christ's-sake, did much more and by that he attracted large crowds of people.

When Metropolitan Filaret saw, on the one hand, that pilgrims constantly massed near the porch of his cottage, impatiently waiting for the appearance of the beloved Starets Feofil, and, on the other hand he did not wish to cause himself and those with him the daily distractions of Feofil's actions, he no longer tried to keep the Starets with him. He finally called Feofil in after the morning tea and said:

"Well, brother Feofil, God blesses you. Get ready old sparrow, for your former nest in Kitayev. You will be freer there."

"Direct my steps according to your word," answered Feofil, as he had always said when he was to be moved from one place to another, and having diligently prayed before the icons, he set out on the indicated path.

The Blessed One returned to Kitayev and lived there peacefully for a long time. No one complained about his way of life again and no one tried to end his foolish escapades. The hidden light was again placed on the candle-stand and began to shine on everyone.

IX

It is said that the Blessed One's dislike of money was amazing. The Starets was tied to nothing. He never took money, or if he did accept it on the strong request of the zealous, he would give it all away to the poor and wretched. One generous noblewoman offered him a sizable sum for distributing to the poor. Not wishing to offend her by refusing, the Blessed One accepted her gift but as soon as she had departed, he threw the money out the door of his cell and thus set his mind at rest. This action was seen by greedy ones who, taking advantage of the Starets' simpleness, pocketed the gold.

Countess Orlova-Chesmenskaya once met Feofil at the gates of the Lavra and asked:

"Father Feofil! I am going away today. Tell me, what can I buy you as a keepsake?"

The Starets glanced at her, smiled, and gave her some cryptic reply. Orlova did not understand his words but when she asked others about this, it became clear that the Starets had asked that he be brought a shtoff (1.2 litres) of vodka. By this answer, he gave her to understand that all earthly possessions and gifts were as disdainful for him as a shtoff of vodka.

Another time, the tender-hearted Abbess Agnia of the Kievo-Florovsky Monastery heard that the Starets often prayed standing on the damp ground of the woods and she felt sorry for him.

"My God! How is it that he spends entire days on damp ground, praying for us sinners? We must give this pious man a little rug."

She ordered her cell-mates to sew a fine rug and when it was finished, she sent it to the Blessed One through his own sister, the postulant, Anna Novichkova. The Starets accepted the rug in order not to offend Agnia. But on the following day he set out for the woods, took the little rug with him, spread it on the ground, sat on it for a minute or two and then threw it aside and departed, leaving the rug behind on the grass. Understandably, someone soon took the abandoned gift since it was of excellent quality. The Starets, however, quickly ceased even thinking about it.

Among Feofil's admirers were two high-ranking field officers, Mikhail Dmitrievich Pozdniak, an officer in the Kiev administration of the Governor-General, and his friend, also a brilliant officer. Every week on Sundays and holidays, the two of them would visit the Starets, have dinner in his cell and spend the entire day in soul-saving talks.

Once, these two friends decided to play a harmless joke on the Blessed One. They secretly took his worn out schema vestments and ordered new ones in the city. The Starets was extemely grieved and regretted the loss, and when the two culprits of the theft personally brought him both the old and the new schemas, he said with a smile:

"Jokers! What did you do this for? Don't you see that you have almost led me into sin? I began to prepare for prayers to the King, but I didn't have my schema. I wanted to perform a service in church, but I didn't have my schema. Glory to God that you have at least returned my old one."

"But put on the new one! Your old one isn't suitable."

"Mockers! Who would appear to be reviewed by the Tsar without wearing his decorations and full regalia? What rewards have I merited in this new schema, while on the old one some things even stand in beauty?"

Not putting on the new schema even once, he sent it to the vestry of the Far Caves.

And here is an example of the secret charity of the Blessed One.

There lived in the Lavra a postulant who was serving his obedience in the Novopasechny orchard. Upon attaining his maturity, he was called into the military service as a recruit. He was judged suitable for service and inducted. The young ascetic of piety was overwhelmed with grief at his impending separation from the cloister. He could not buy his way out of the service, because he had no money. (At that time, a recruit could pay for his obligated service instead of serving himself. This cost up to 1,000 rubles).

He happened to meet Starets Feofil soon after this and the Blessed One looked at him intently and said:

"Why have you become sad, soldier? Because you don't want to serve the earthly king? You want to become employed for service to the Heavenly King?"

"Oh, I'm not worthy of this mercy from God. There is no place for me a sinner, in this holy cloister of the Lavra," the postulant said and tears poured from his eyes like hail.

"Well, well, don't weep, don't grieve, brother. You will remain living in the Lavra," the Blessed One said, and went on his way.

Three days later, Countess Orlova-Chesmenskaya came to Kiev on a pilgrimage and, having finished her podvig of worship, she went to see Starets Feofil in order to take confession with him. She did not find him in his cell but seeing Feofil in the courtyard, she set out towards him. Having guessed Orlova's intention, the Blessed One decided to test her humility and, as if he had not noticed her, he quickly set out for the woods. Orlova did not wish to lose sight of the Starets because it was not always easy to find him, so she began to follow him. The Starets increased his pace. Orlova did the same. Making sharp turns and detours so that Orlova would lose sight of him, Feofil would again appear in the distance. The Blessed One was heading for the Novopasechny orchard and, having entered the wicket-gate, he quickly disappeared from her view.

The anxious countess had lost Feofil's track and so she stopped in confusion. To her good fortune, that same postulant-recruit was sitting near the gate and she walked up to him with the question:

"Tell me, please. Did Father Feofil pass through here?"

"He has just entered the orchard," the postulant replied, bowing respectfully and he opened the gate in front of the countess. "Allow me... "

Forgetting herself from joy, Orlova took a handful of gold coins from her purse and gave it to the postulant in gratitude.

The money was not only sufficient for the paying out of the recruit's service requirement, but there was some left over for his other needs as well.

Starets Feofil was so famous in the Kiev region that hardly a single simple, pious, and God-loving person in the area would begin his own affairs without first seeking the advice and direction of the Starets. Rarely would a wedding begin without his blessing. Each person would accept, without question, the word of the Starets, even if it was stern and uncomfortable for the hearer, and they would carry out his advice in exactness, as a prophetic voice from heaven.

There lived in Kiev a broker, Ivan N. In his youth, when he was serving as a salesman in some store, he had decided to marry. For a long time he searched for the girl of his dreams, and then, at a merchants' convention, his gaze lighted on Liubochka Z. The broker's fate was decided. He would propose to Liubochka. He got dressed in his finest clothing, went to her parents' home and declared his intentions. He received this answer from the girl's mother:

"Our Liubochka is already engaged. Her fiance is the young man Hendrick M. Although he is of the Lutheran faith, we cannot go back on our given word. . . "

"Oh, my God! But I love your daughter madly!"

"Well, what can be done? It's a pity that you did not speak of this earlier."

The broker was a very intelligent, business-like person, while the German was flighty but rich. Liubocka's parents, hearing the proposal of the broker, gathered their relatives to their home and held a consultation but the majority of them spoke in favour of the German. But before arranging the wedding, they decided to visit Starets Feofil. They brought some rolls, bread, incense, and candles and set out for the cell of the Blessed One. When they arrived, the Starets opened the door for them and welcomed everyone, but, not allowing the visitors to utter a word, he said:

"Ivan, Ivan. Don't dare to give her away to that blockhead Hendrick!"

The parents heeded, Liubochka married the broker and was happy all her life.

And there was another occasion. The widowed landowner, Fekla Tarasova, had a beautiful young daughter, Anna. Two suitors sought her in marriage. One was handsome, stately, good-natured, and prone to drink and carouse. The other had a small pox scarred face and was sullen, but of gentle and reliable nature. The first lived in Dimievka, a suburb of Kiev, the second, in the little town of Myshelovka. Anna was madly in love with the handsome one but totally indifferent towards the second one and refused point-blank to marry him. Her mother, on the other hand, insisted that she marry the one from Myshelovka.

They set out to Kitayev for the Starets' advice. The Blessed One, saying not a word, gave Anna a yoke with pails and ordered her to bring some water from Dimievka. The maiden fulfilled the order. The Blessed One poured the water into a barrel standing under the drain-pipe and again gave Anna the pails with an order to go to Myshelovka for water this time. The water was brought in half an hour.

"Where was it more difficult to bring it from?" the Starets asked the maiden.

"From Dimievka," Anna answered. "It is far from here, but it is closer to Myshelovka."

"Well remember then. The pails on the shoulder represent your life. If you listen to your mother and marry the one from

Myshelovka, then your life will be light. But if you marry the one from Dimievka, you will curse your entire life from woe and needs."

Convinced by these words, Anna heeded her mother's advice and, having married the man from Myshelovka, she never repented this in her entire life.

But once it was just the opposite. The Starets advised a youth to marry a certain young widow, but the young man married a maiden whom he himself had chosen.

"Why bother listening to such an old man?" he said to his comrades. "The old monk won't find out anyway."

When, in a week's time the young couple came to Kitayev, they went to see the Starets for his blessing. Feofil met them on the threshold of his cell and instead of his blessing, the newly-weds received an old, worn out basket, on the bottom of which was a pile of rubbish and on top lay two apples. Not being able to understand this, the young people went to the Kitayev spiritual father for an explanation. The spiritual father listened to them and said:

"Two fresh apples — that is you. The pile of rubbish under them —that is the unfortunate life under you."

And, in fact, not even a year passed before the young couple began to quarrel and finally separated.

X

We have related several cases and examples in the previous chapters which have convinced us of the reality of the gift of forevision possessed by Starets Feofil and of how wisely and exactly he used this gift for the advice and correction of the souls of vain and sinful mankind. In addition to these aforementioned incidents, we present here a few more cases of the gift of forevision of the Blessed One.

1. On the morning of August 14, 1852, the Blessed One set out in his cart from Kitayev to the Lavra. It was the eve of the Feast of the Dormition and Feofil intended to spend a night and a day there. As he was passing through the forest near the place where the Preobrazhenskaya Hermitage now stands, the bullock turned to the right as if it were lost, but the Starets, occupied with reading the psalter, did not seem to notice this and so the bullock continued on his way into the dense woods. Some men with axes who were walking from the nearest village noticed this error and began crying out to the Starets:

"Batiushka! Your bullock is lost. Look — he's not going in the right direction."

The Blessed One seemed to tear himself away from reading the Psalter, then turned to the men and said:

"Let him go his way. He knows better than we do what he needs there. It is done so that I can pray to God in this place."

With these words, the Starets got out of his wagon, took an axe from one of the men, cut down a small tree and hewed a small cross from it. At that time the whole area around where the Preobrazhenskaya Hermitage now stands was dense woods and thoughts about building in it had never even entered anyone's mind. Never-the-less, the Blessed Feofil, foreseeing in spirit the future grace of the place, prayed to God and as once Andrew-the-First-Called had erected a cross on the heights of Kiev, so the Blessed Starets now planted his cross on this spot and said:

"Remember, friends! On this spot a monastery will be built and many of the living and the dead will settle in it."

What was foretold was fulfilled. In 1872, at the place where Feofil had erected his cross, the beginnings of the Preobrazhenskaya Hermitage was built, and aside from living people, seeking peace for their souls, the dead were laid to rest there for their eternal peace, in expectation of the approaching day of God's fearful judgement.

2. The Blessed One foretold the following concerning the founding of the Holy Trinity-Ionovsky Monastery.

On the Samburg farm of the Kitayevskaya Hermitage lived the postulant nun, Pelagia. She felt a sincere veneration towards the Starets and lovingly fulfilled any obedience the Blessed One might give her. If he told her to have a shirt washed, she would wash it; if he told her to harness the bullock, she would go to harness it; if he sent her to the Dnieper to wash a pair of boots, she would do so. Because of her constant service and simple obedience, the Starets loved the postulant very much and would often protect her from various temptations and troubles.

Once, a starets-hieroschemamonk from Mount Athos came to the Lavra and offered to secretly tonsure Pelagia and three other postulants of the farm. Not wishing to accept this tempting offer without the blessing of Starets Feofil, the postulants went to him for advice. The Blessed One did not say a word to them but brought out a loaf without the inside and said:

"Your thoughts are as empty as this bread," and he forbade Pelagia to be confused by vainglorious thoughts.

Another time the Starets called her to himself and gave her a bottle. "Go and buy yourself some honey, incense, and candles," he said, "and remember the number 12."

Pelagia did as she was told and as she was returning, the Starets met her near the market, surrounded by many people.

"Well, did you buy it?" he asked.

"I bought it, Batiushka," answered Pelagia.

"Well then, begin praying for my father and I will pray for your father right now."

And he began to prostrate himself in the middle of the street. Pelagia was embarrassed. People were standing all around, as if looking at some marvel, but having overcome her embarrassment, she too began to make prostrations.

Several days passed. Suddenly Pelagia received a letter from her relatives that on the twelfth of that month, her father had died after an illness.

But let us return to the aim of our story. Starets Feofil once met Pelagia on the road and ordered her to take the bullock by the rope and lead it to the Lavra while he himself turned around in the wagon towards the east and began his usual reading of the Psalter. As they were going beyond Zberints, at the place where the Holy Trinity-Ionovsky Monastery now stands, the Blessed One stopped the bullock and told his fellow traveler to give it some hay. Then he called her to himself and said:

"Pelagia! If you threw a large seine net into the depths of the Dnieper, what would you pull out?"

"Everything, Batiuska," Pelagia answered, having thought about it. "Both large and tiny fish. There would be pike, and carp, and roach in it, and mussels and frogs as well."

"Well, then, know that on this spot God's grace will soon shine and a large monastery will be built on it. And as in the seine of the fisherman there is found everything, so in this young cloister not all will be the same in spiritual growth. There will appear in it 'pike' of high ascetic life, and there will also steal into it worthless 'shells', little caring for the purity of the soul."

And raising his eyes to heaven, the Starets blessed the place in all four directions and, having prayed for half an hour, he continued on his way to the Lavra.

And now, today, when the prophecy of the Blessed Starets has been fulfilled in all accuracy, and, in place of the shifting sands, we see a beautiful, well-built monastery, our minds automatically recall the prophetic words:

"The wilderness and the solitary place shall be glad... And the desert shall rejoice, and blossom as a rose...It shall blossom abundantly and rejoice...; they shall see the glory of the Lord and the excellency of our God" (Is. 35:1-2).

3. The Blessed One was walking along the shore of the Dnieper to the Lavra. His cell-mate, Panteleimon, was with him. It was about two hours before the church bells begin to ring. Coming to the place where the Lavra caves dominate the hill, the Starets saw a boat tied on the shore of the Dnieper and said:

"Do you know what I've thought of, Panteleimon?"

"What is that, Batiushka?"

"Let us both go over to the other side of the Dnieper. No one over there is praying to God, so we'll pray for everyone and then read the holy Psalter."

"As you wish, Batiushka."

The two came up to the shore and the Blessed One untied the boat which was without an oar, then told Panteleimon to sit down in it.

"But how will we go?" the cell-mate asked him in bewilderment. "There is no oar, Batiushka. I will run for an oar; there is a guard house nearby."

"No need. Sit down, I tell you."

"But what about the oar? Or will we use our hands?"

"What do you need an oar for, you simpleton?"

"To move ahead in the water. To steer the boat."

"Sit down! Sit down! The Lord directs the whole world and He will direct our little shell."

Panteleimon sat down and watched to see what would happen next. The Blessed One pushed the little boat away from the shore, seated himself in the stern and opened his Psalter.

"Bless, O Lord!" he said and immersed himself in his reading.

And what a miracle! The boat peacefully went ahead by itself. Panteleimon sat amazed and breathless. He could not utter a single word. The ripples of the river rocked the frail vessel. The sun was warmly shining and a gentle breeze was blowing. The distance to the opposite shore grew less.

Suddenly, something flashed before the eyes of the cell-mate. From the water lept several gold fish and, landing in the bottom of the boat, they began to play about, their scales brightly sparkling in the sun. Panteleimon glanced at the Blessed Starets in utter bewilderment.

"Silence! Be quiet!" the Blessed One said. "These are God's angels. The Lord has sent them for our consolation."

Panteleimon entered an indescribable rapture and sat staring at the fish. As the boat began to near the shore, the fish lept over the side and disappeared into the depths.

On the return trip, the very same thing occurred.

"Guard your lips," said the Starets to his cell-mate as they left the banks of the Dniepr, "and place a barrier to your mouth. See that you do not tell anyone about what you saw until after I die."

Panteleimon kept all this in great secret until the demise of the Blessed Starets and only after his repose did he begin to tell about this miracle to many of the Lavra brothers.

Marvelous is the Lord, Who creates all that He wants on earth, in the seas, and in all the depths. In His hands are the depths of the earth and the heights of the mountains. The sea is His for He created it.

4. Another incident which the cell-mate related is no less amazing.

The Starets had been moved to the Goloseyevskaya Hermitage. One day in May of 1853, about six months before his death, the Blessed One said to his cell-mate:

"Panteleimon! Let us go into the woods and pray to God."

As they walked, the Starets read the Gospel, sang the psalms, and knitted a stocking, while Panteleimon cut hay along the way and gathered it into a net in order to treat the bullock on their return home. They walked an exceptionally long way, and when evening came on and the sun began to set, the travellers turned homeward. Walking past the place where the Preobrazhenskaya Hermitage now stands, the Starets stopped and said:

"How about resting on this hill for a while, Panteleimon, and feasting our eyes on the view of the holy Lavra?"

The weary cell-mate was just waiting for this and he spread out on the grass and began to doze off. Starets Feofil took out a piece of ice, put it in water and added some honey and drank it in order to strengthen his exhausted body. Half an hour passed. Suddenly, the Blessed One cried:

"Panteleimon! Some strangers are approaching. Run out and call them here."

The drowsy cell-mate raised his head and saw a group of pilgrims coming down the road. He called them over to the Starets.

"May God help you!" the Blessed One greeted them.

"Thank you, Batiushka," the men replied.

"Perhaps you haven't had anything to eat yet?" asked Feofil.

"Hardly, Batiushka. We've chewed on some dried bread crusts in water but there has been no hot food on our tongue for a whole week."

"Never mind. Sit down and chat for a while. The Mother of God will feed everyone at once."

Then, having seated the travellers, the Blessed One took a small cast-iron tripod out of his basket, dug a small hole in the ground, and sent Panteleimon out to gather some twigs.

"Twigs?! What good will they do to you, Batiushka!" the bewildered cell-mate responded, knowing that there was nothing to cook.

"Simpleton!" the Blessed One chided him. "We'll boil gruel. You see, it is necessary to feed the pilgrims."

The twigs were brought but there was still no fire.

"What trouble!" Panteleimon exclaimed with annoyance. "There is nothing to start a fire with, Batiushka."

"And God?!" the Starets said impressively.

Then raising his eyes, he began to pray:

"O Lord! At Thy command, fire goes before Thee and lightning illumines the heavens. Hear, O Lord, the voice of my prayers when I call unto Thee, when I raise my hands to Thy holy temple. Hear my supplications; may the poor eat and be filled and praise Thy All-Blessed Name!"

With these words, he prostrated to the east and then blessed the little tripod. saying, "In the name of the Father, and the Son, and the Holy Spirit. . . "

But barely had he finished these words when, from under the tripod, a wisp of blue smoke appeared. The twigs began to smoke and soon burst into bright flames.

Upon seeing such a miracle, Panteleimon wanted to run but the Starets stopped him and, wagging his finger, he ordered him to throw some short grass into the pot while he himself dropped in several pebbles and a piece of ice taken from the basket. When all this began to boil, the Blessed One, not interrupting his mental prayer, blessed the tripod once more and mixed the contents of the pot.

"Well, taste it now," he said, turning to his cell-mate.

Panteleimon scooped out a bit of the gruel on the end of a spoon and carefully licked it with his tongue. Then he scooped up a whole spoonful and ate it.

"Batiushka! !" he cried out in astonishment. "Really and truly, it's semolina."

"Hurry and pour it out for the guests, simpleton, before it gets cold."

The cell-mate, joyously and with fear, seized the pot and began to ladle out the gruel into the travelling cups of the dumbfounded pilgrims. But no matter how much he poured out, the amount of gruel in the pot did not lessen. Everyone had been provided for and had eaten his fill, but the pot remained full. Just as the loaves and fishes were multiplied in the wilderness to feed the multitude, so also was the gruel now multiplied in answer to the prayers of Starets Feofil.

"Well, God be with you," said the Blessed One gently, turning to the travellers when they had finished eating. "Go to the holy Lavra and pray for everyone."

Completely staggered by the miracle they had just witnessed with their own eyes, the pilgrims set out for the Lavra and there began to tell everyone, with joy and fear of the miracle.

For all that you ask in prayer, with true faith, you will receive.

5. On July 5, 1853, at 8 A.M., Abbess Seraphima of the Kievo-Florovsky Monastery and the nun Agnia, her treasurer, arrived at the Lavra in order to petition Metropolitan Filaret to serve a

liturgy in their cloister on the feast day of its church, which was named in honour of the Kazan Icon of the Mother of God.

Vladika received the visitors warmly and agreed to accept their invitation with pleasure.

"Good, good, " he said. "I will definitely be there. Just prepare all that is necessary for the service."

The Abbess then started to take leave of the Metropolitan, but he detained her.

"Are you planning to return home now, honorable Mother?"

"Well, yes, we had planned to, Your Eminence."

"But I am serving a special liturgy today in the St. Sergei Church at the Kitayevskaya Hermitage. By good fortune you are here and so perhaps you would consent to joining us for the service?"

"Your blessing, holy Vladika. With great pleasure."

The Metropolitan began rushing to get ready for the journey, but, to his great chagrin, he could not find his prayer rope.

"Oh, what a grief you are," Vladika said to himself. "You must have forgotten the prayer rope and left it at Goloseyev-skaya."

He called to his cell-mate, Father Nazary, but Seraphima interjected:

"Perhaps you could use mine, Vladika?"

"Yours? But what will you do for a prayer rope? They say that it is a bad omen to go without it, but what else is to be done. Let me use yours."

The Abbess gave her prayer rope to Vladika and then, leaving him to finish his preparations, she set out ahead for Kitayev with Sister Agnia.

On that day the Kitayevskaya Hermitage was in a great bustle. The Metropolitan had informed them of his arrival quite late and the sextons, taken unawares, were rushing about in all directions sweeping, cleaning, and preparing vestments, while the sacristan and the superior of the hermitage had worked themselves into complete exhaustion. In order not to miss the arrival of the Vladika, watches had been sent to the belfry at dawn. At that time the higher clergy always travelled in carriages drawn by four horses, and the sentries were just waiting for such a foursome to appear.

Suddenly, one of the watches sighted the four-horse carriage of the Florovsky abbess approaching in the distance, and assuming that it was Metropolitan Filaret's carriage, with the exuberance peculiar to young postulants, cried out, "He is coming!"

The bell-ringer was just waiting for this and, with a strong, skilled hand, he began ringing the bells with all his might.

The brothers quickly poured out of the church with banners, cross, and holy water and stood waiting to receive Vladika. The four-horse carriage drove up, the coachman stopped his team, but instead of the expected Metropolitan, out stepped Abbess Serafima of the Florovsky Monastery. There was some confusion, but matters were soon set in order again.

Soon, the Metropolitan arrived and the liturgy was served with the proper ceremony. The church and the monastery yard were especially crowded due to the influx of summer residents in the neighborhood and a large crowd of pilgrims from the Lavra. The Blessed Feofil took part in the liturgy and service of thanksgiving and according to his custom, during the liturgy, he stood apart from the other celebrants, half-turned aside. After the liturgy, the Metropolitan began to bless the people and Abbess Seraphima, together with Sister Agnia, set out for the gate in order to go home.

While they were walking along the side of the church, Feofil met them and not answering Seraphima's greetings, he pulled a bottle of sand out of his pocket and poured it on her from head to toe.

Seraphima cried out in fright and unhappily hurried to the gate with her co-traveller. But just as they were seating themselves in the carriage, Ivan, Feofil's cell-mate, ran up to them and gave Agnia a long woman's gown, inside of which was tied a whole sheaf of rye.

"Oh, my God! What is this?" said Agnia, flinching back.

"Don't be afraid," answered the cell-mate. "Batiushka Feofil sent this. He said,'Tell Agnia to remove the heads and keep them, but to send the straws back to me'."

Agnia accepted the gift with great confusion and put it inside the carriage. The coachman waved his whip and sent the horses forward.

What did the Blessed One foretell with these strange actions?

Immediately upon returning home, Seraphima felt unwell and towards evening became ill and went to bed. By the time the Kazan feast day arrived and the Metropolitan came to serve the liturgy, she was so ill that she could not rise from her bed.

When Vladika found out about Seraphima's sudden illness, he was extremely saddened. "Preserve her, Oh God," he said with unhidden sorrow. "She is so young and full of life and now she has become ill. Pray for her, sisters in Christ, pray fervently and may the Lord preserve her safely and unharmed." He then turned to the Governor-General, Prince Vasilchikov, who was a fine example of a true and God-loving son of the Church, and said, "Let us go and confort her."

When they arrived in her cell, the ill one was lying motionless. Seeing the presence of her high ranking visitors, she moved and wanted to rise from the bed, but the Vladika forbade her to strain herself.

"The prayer rope, do you remember the prayer rope?" he asked the ill abbess in a saddened voice. "My little observation about the omen has come about. Yes, it has come about."

Having given the ill one a holy blessing, he wished her a speedy recovery and left the cell. Towards evening Seraphima became much worse and on July 10, on the Feast of St. Antony of Pechersk, she felt herself coming to life's end. She ordered a carriage to be sent to the Lavra to bring her spiritual father, Hieroschemamonk Parfeny. When the Starets came to her with the Holy Gifts, it was already too late. Abbess Seraphima had already yielded up her soul.

On July 12, the treasurer, Agnia,[2] was elected to replace the deceased abbess. And so, the prophecy of the Blessed Starets came to pass.

6.   At 7 P.M. on September 13, 1851, His Majesty, Emperor Nikolai Pavlovich, together with the Grand Dukes Nikolai Nikolaevich and Mikhail Nikolaevich, entered Kiev.[3] Since it was already dark, and because His Majesty was travelling on the Zhitomir road from Lusk, and the Lavra did not lie on his route, he was unable to visit it that evening. Instead, he went directly to his apartment at the home of the military governor. On the following day, September 14, which was the Feast of the Elevation of the Cross, the imperial travellers attended the Lavra liturgy which was served by Metropolitan Filaret. Then at 10:45 there was a review of the troops on the Esplanade Square from where His Majesty continued to St. Sophia Cathedral. From there, he proceeded to the Mikhailovsky Monastery, after which he viewed the city, the newly erected fortifications and other buildings and the arsenal.

On September 15, His Majesty, together with the Granl Dukes, left to review the troops in Elisavetgrad.

At noon, on September 19, Nikolai Pavlovich returned to Kiev alone, leaving the two Grand Dukes behind. At 2:30 P.M., accompanied by the Governor-General and military engineers, he examined the fortification works and walked from the new (Nikolsky) gates to the yard of the engineers' command and past the Lavra stables which were situated near the Nikolsky Monastery (often called "Little Nikolai") to the military cathedral (the "Great Nikolai"). Having examined the cathedral, His Majesty said to the dean who had greeted him:

"It is a good cathedral. It should be restored."

Then, pointing to the iconostas which was darkened with age, he asked who had built it. The protopriest replied that it was built by Hetman Mazepa in 1690.

The Sovereign said, "He is cursed here, but he is also prayed for here, in order that God may forgive him."

Then the Tsar pointed out some icons which were hung along the walls in such a way that the people were required to stand with their backs to them and he ordered that they be moved nearer to the iconostas or placed in the sanctuary.

From the military cathedral, His Majesty set out for the tomb of Askold which, according to the decision of the city planners, was to be dug up to make way for a new access route to the bridge on the main highway. The Sovereign ordered that the plans be altered so that the highway would pass by the tomb and spare the entire cemetery which was around it. Then Nikolai Pavlovich continued to inspect the fortress and citadel until 3:30 at which time the Sovereign entered his carriage and, accompanied by his suite, engineers, and city authorities, set out for his quarters. Then a most unusual and significant event took place.

As the carriage was driving through Perchersk, and about to turn a corner, His Imperial Majesty met with Feofil who came plodding around the corner on his bullock. No sooner did the Tsar's horses come even with Feofil's cart than they stopped as if they had suddenly become frozen to the ground. All the efforts of the coachman to make the horses proceed were in vain. The horses strained to the right and to the left but they could not move the carriage from its spot.

Seeing the monk in a ragged cloak near him, the Sovereign became interested in finding out who he was. The Tsar's suite and the city authorities quickly rushed to Feofil and brought him to the Sovereign's carriage.

"What kind of person are you?" Nikolai Pavlovich sternly asked Feofil, taking him in with a penetrating glance.

"I am a man of God," the Blessed One replied with child-like simplicity.

Emperor Nikolai Pavlovich of Russia

"I know you are God's, but where do you come from and where are you going?"

"Where I am from — I am there no longer. Where I am now — everyone can see. Where I will be later — God alone knows."

Nikolai Pavlovich gave a questioning look to his suite and they, extremely embarrassed by Feofil's reply, hastened to explain that this simple person was the monk Feofil, a fool-for-Christ's-sake, of the Kievo-Pecherskaya Lavra.

"A God's fool-monk?" asked Nikolai Pavlovich with amazement. "Strange."

But wishing to end the embarrassment of those accompanying him, he kindly turned to Feofil and said:

"Well, go with God and wish me a happy journey."

"No, Your Majesty. You have to go through thorns," the Blessed One answered to this, peacefully climbing into his cart.

At that very moment the horses strained to one side and the Tsar's carriage sped ahead. The Sovereign heard these prophetically significant words of Starets Feofil and looked back intently at the strange monk.

On the morning of September 20, the Tsar unexpectedly visited the Lavra and without any welcoming, he entered the cathedral church where the liturgy was taking place and "It is meet to praise Thee" was being sung. After the usual parting prayers, the Sovereign, having eliminated the ceremonial "seeing off" from the church to the holy gate, accepted the Metropolitan's blessing and set out for St. Petersburg.

In 1852, Emperor Nikolai Pavlovich visited, for the last time, the city which was dear to his heart, not long before the beginning of the war with Turkey which led to the unfortunate Crimean campaign and placed the Sovereign in his untimely grave. The Tsar arrived in Kiev at 11 A.M. on Sunday, October 5, accompanied by the Grand Dukes Nikolai Nikolaevich and Mikhail Nikolaevich.

At 1 P.M. the Sovereign went to the Lavra where he visited the Metropolitan and conversed with him in his private chambers. The Tsar was extremely sullen and unhappy. His brow furrowed and his gaze clouded with constant thought, Nikolai Pavlovich recalled the Christians in the East who were being protected by him, and who were now again being oppressed by the Turks. The heart of the Russian Tsar, softened by prayer in the church, was filled with pity for the unfortunate sufferers. He also recalled how the Turks had formerly oppressed the Slavs and the Greeks and how the Russian Sovereigns had tried to lighten their sufferings and even he, Nikolai Pavlovich, had to declare a bloody war. The Turks were defeated then and asked for peace and Greece was recognized as an independent state. Now they were again beginning to oppress the Christians under their power and again were forcing the Tsar to declare war against them. But now the strength of the Turks was being multiplied threefold — the English and the French, wishing to weaken the strength of Russia, were preparing to help them. At the end of the conversation, the Sovereign, as if hinting to Vladika about the alarming state of the political affairs, expressed that a menacing cloud was spreading over the fatherland, but that he was doing all in his power to prevent the dear native land from being stained and to deal with the enemies in dignity.

"I do not want to shed the blood of the faithful sons of my fatherland needlessly, but our vainglorious enemies are forcing me to bare my sword. My plans are not yet made — no! But my heart feels that the time is nearing and they will soon be brought to fulfilment."

After these words, the Sovereign sadly lowered his head and fell into deep thought.

"Oh, how I would like to know what awaits Russia in the future," he continue after some silence.

"But no-one knows this except God alone," the Metropolitan remarked with a sigh.

"Yes, I know that it is so ," replied the Sovereign. "But I also know that the Holy Kievo-Pecherskaya Lavra, which has from time immemorial served as a seed-bed of faith and piety, was always rich with pious monks who have carried within themselves the spirit of truly ascetic life. Do you not have any elders who are filled with spiritual grace and whom I might ask for advice on my forthcoming political projects?"

"There is, Your Majesty," the Metropolitan replied. "There is such a one. And although his mode of life in no way resembles the model of life of the other monks of the monastery, I can assure Your Imperial Majesty with confidence, that under the cover of his simplicity and foolishness there is hidden the grace of the Holy Spirit and an undoubted gift of forevision."

"Is it that tall monk whom I met once in the city? As nearly as I can remember, he was riding on a cart pulled by a bullock."

"That is correct, Your Majesty," answered the Vladika Metropolitan. "That is he, Schemamonk Feofil. If it would be pleasing to Your Imperial Majesty, I will not hesitate to present him before you. He lives in the Kitayevskaya Hermitage and within an hour my carriage could have him here."

"No, it is not necessary. We will go there ourselves. That would be much better."

It was settled that they would leave for the Kitayevskaya Hermitage immediately after dinner. At the agreed time, the Tsar and Vladika set out in the Metropolitan's carriage to visit Feofil.

And what did the Blessed One do? In spite of the fact that a messenger had arrived at Kitayev from the Metropolitan with orders to keep Starets Feofil at the monastery all day, the elder managed to slip through the gate and into the woods. Seeing in spirit the nearing of the Tsar's carriage, he went out to meet it in Goloseyevo. Running through the bushes and scratching his hands and face into bloodiness, he found a large ant-hill some distance from the road. He dug into it with his hands and lay down in the middle of it on his back.

The weather that day was sunny and warm and the drive was very pleasant, but all the while the Tsar was silent and in deep thought, looking about the surrounding countryside, pointing to an object which had caught his eye. "A dead body, or what?"

Vladika looked in the direction in which the Tsar was pointing, but his aging eyes could not see what was lying there.

"Gavril!" he turned to his valet who was sitting in the coach-box. "Have a look brother."

"There is a man lying there, Your Eminence," Gavrilka answered, turning around. "But he is not dead, he's alive. See there, his feet are moving."

"What is he lying on?" the Sovereign asked.

"It would seem that he is lying on an ant-hill, Your Imperial Majesty," answered Gavrilka.

"Strange," said the Tsar to this and ordered the coachman to turn off to the side.

When the travellers got out of the carriage and approached the ant-hill, Feofil was lying there, not moving. His arms were folded on his chest crosswise, as in death, and his eyes were completely closed. Ants swarmed in masses all over his body and face, but he, as if feeling nothing, pretended to be dead.

"This is Schemamonk Feofil," the Metropolitan quietly whispered to the Sovereign and walked up closer. "This is that very starets whom we are going to visit."

"Why is he lying here?" Nikolai Pavlovich asked in amazement. "Find out, won't you?"

"Feofil!" Vladika bent towards the Blessed One. "Why are you lying here?"

Silence.

"Get up, I tell you, you culprit! The Sovereign wants to talk to you."

Neither sound nor movement.

"Strange!" said the Sovereign with annoyance and, angrily waving his hand, he turned back to the carriage.

"No! This is not to be forgotten without reflection, Your

Imperial Majesty," noted the Metropolitan to the Monarch when they sat down in the carriage. "My heart knows that this prank of his has a very deep significance."

But no matter how hard Vladika tried to reason out the meaning of the Staret's behaviour for the Sovereign, he could not give a clear, positive answer.

Some time elapsed and the war with Turkey was declared. On September 2, 1854, the allied fleet pulled in to the shores of the Crimea and landed a large army of about 70,000 English, French, and Turkish troops. The Russian troops were comparatively few in number, but never-the-less, they stood and fought. Russian sailors sank a part of their own fleet in the entrance to Sevastopol Bay in order to block the way of the enemy fleet and they carried cannons from the ships to the shore to form a battery. The naval forces became infantry and prepared for the desperate defence under the heroic leadership of admirals Kornilov, Nakhimov, Istomin, and others.

The enemy approached. Sevastopol, as a maritime city, was not fortified from the land. But the Russians did not lose spirit and in several days they erected earthen fortifications for a distance of seven versts. They worked day and night. The troops were helped by the inhabitants, not excluding women and children who carried earth for the embankments. One battery was erected exclusively by women for which it was named "The Maidens".

War began. Bombs, shells, and shot fell like hail from both sides. From early morning until late at night the enemy fire did not cease. The entire world marvelled at the staunchness and extraordinary bravery of the Russian troops. But the Russian forces became thinned out as the lines of the valiant defenders fell. The cemetery grew. Emperor Nikolai Pavlovich, depressed with sorrow, became noticeably thin. His health began to break up from worries and troubles. Finally, he caught a severe cold and took to his bed.

And then, at the beginning of the Battle of Sinope, the news arrived from the battle front of the unbelievable losses of Russian forces and even of such heroes as Nakhimov and Kornilov — all this completely broke the heart of the Sovereign. On Feb. 18, 1855, Tsar Nikolai Pavlovich peacefully demised, having been tormented with worries and worn with sorrow.

The venerable Archpastor wept openly when he received the staggering news of the death of the beloved Monarch, for no-one felt more affection and love for the deceased Sovereign than did Metropolitan Filaret.

"We no longer have our very own father in Russia," the Metropolitan said to his cell-mate, Father Sergei, his voice quivering with sorrow. "We will no longer see him in our holy monastery; no longer will we admire his strong step; we will not hear his royal voice or see his shining eyes."

After these words, the Metropolitan called his valet, Gavrila Feodorovich Golushka, and said:

"Do you remember, Gavril, our trip with the Sovereign to Kitayev? And do you remember the ant-hill and Feofil on it?"

"How could I forget, holy Vladika, even though that was three years ago."

"Take note, then, that up to now I could not understand his strange behaviour. Now, the prophecy of the Starets is as clear as God's day. The ants were the malicious enemies of our fatherland, trying to torment the great body of Russia. The arms folded on his chest and the closed eyes of Feofil were the sudden, untimely death of our beloved Batiushka-Tsar."

XI

On April 23, 1853, not long before his demise, Blessed Feofil was once more moved to Goloseyevo. This was done at the request of the superior of the Goloseyevskaya Hermitage who had a great love and respect for the Starets and felt that the aged monk would be more comfortable at Goloseyevo.

"Let it be as you wish," the Starets replied to the kind invitation of the superior. "I'll return to my old place to die."

These words were prophetic. On July 15, of that same year, three months before his death, Starets Feofil, on the orders of the Metropolitan, again returned to Kitayev.

During the last days of his earthly life, the Blessed One began to weaken noticeably, but not wishing to yield to his bodily weaknesses, the Starets avoided all rest and comforted himself with thoughts of God and with prayers, finding in them a singular source of strength and consolation. No sooner would his physical sufferings begin to oppress him than he would turn to his prayers and would be immediately restored in soul and strengthened in body. Thus, not changing his mode of life or his habits, Blessed Feofil continued to live as before. His life continued to be characterized by a meek temper, silent lips, humble heart, a spirit of tender emotion and chastity. His body was subjected to diligent toil, coarse food, a hard bed, tattered clothing, a stuffy cell and physical illness — a source of joy to his soul. Sorrow, deprivation, and need for the sake of the beloved Lord, Jesus Christ.

What a great sea of unselfish love! What a great podvig of humility and human patience! How could he have carried out his deeply instructive example, his face illuminated by the purity of soul, meekness, humility, and simplicity which the Gospels teach? The downward gaze and the brow furrowed with deep thought, clearly testified that his mind was constantly occupied with something else, unseen. Even in the midst of people, the Starets was with God, carried away to heaven in thought. Only those having an understanding of mental activity could see that he prayed in his mind and heart, constantly and without interruption.

The first condition of spiritual life is suffering and the many-sorrowed path of the cross, a struggle with one's self, with the world and with the devil. The Starets had fulfilled this podvig, and the second condition had set in — that of the deep peace and tranquility of a weary soul which, having defeated human passions by means of Christ's grace, was already purified, illuminated, and in secret communication with God. Feofil had found, while still here on earth, the guarantee of future heavenly blessedness. It is impossible for us, sinful people who have not cleansed our hearts of passions, to comprehend the wondrous mystery of this grace-filled condition of the truly righteous soul, for the standards by which we judge in this brief life on earth cannot approach the measure of spiritual grace. It is only possible for us, with true piety, to contemplate a few rays of this bright, God-likeness and purity which, inspite of the efforts of the grace-bearer himself, seem to burst forth in their own unusual actions, words, and movements. Striking into our hearts with spiritual warmth, the grace-bearer affects and subdues our minds with the rare glow of a completely different, higher order of things and draws our souls into this wonderful light of the chosen-one of God.

The character of the life of the Kitayevskaya and Goloseyev-skaya Hermitages was of a patriarchal nature, that is to say, after vespers, all lay persons were required to depart and each brother could settle down freely to pray and worship, each one in his own peaceful corner surrounded by the spirit of saintly fathers of the Lavra. The well-known ascetic, Starets Parfeny, describes Golo-seyevo in these words:

"Here is the spirit of our saintly fathers of the Pecherskaya Lavra. If there is any comfort and joy on earth, it is to be found in the hermitage's silence. People detract us from God, but the hermitage draws us nearer to Him."

Starets Feofil also held such a spiritual opinion and for whole days he would stay in the woods, kneeling on a large stump to pray or else he would go to an ancient hollow oak where he would hang a crucifix and a votive lamp and spend entire days and nights, imitating the podvigs of the ancient stylites. Being thus alone in silence, and being a partaker "of the fellowship that we have. . . with the Father and with His Son Jesus Christ" (I John, 1:3), Feofil would sometimes be seen in the woods completely naked on hot summer days. This he did in order to subject his flesh to the stings of mosquitoes and other insects. Like Adam who,

before his sin, walked about naked and was not ashamed, so Starets
Feofil, adorned with spiritual beauty from above, was not ashamed
of his nakedness.

In the last days of his life, Feofil was often seen in the Lavra
where he went each Saturday to serve an akathist to the Theotokos
before her miraculous icon, the "Chenstokhovskaya Mother of
God."[4] He used to serve this akathist in an extremely original
way. Entering the Great Church, he would seize from the sextons
the first chasuable at hand, vest himself in it, and begin to rush
through the brothers' cells, gathering singers for the kliros. If
any would refuse, he would drive them along with his cane. For
this reason, the akathists which Feofil conducted in the bread-room
where the icon was discovered, were always ceremonious and well
attended.

During the last months of his life, the Starets conversed more
willingly with people and was freer with advice and directions,
beseeching everyone not to forget to pray for the "smelly" Feofil.
His speech revealed a profound knowledge of the Holy Scripture,
the spirit of which he comprehended not only with his mind, but
with a heart enlightened by the grace of God and directed by the
experience of a spiritual life.

"Love one another with a sacred love and do not hold anger
against each other. Do not allow yourselves to be tempted and
avoid attaching your hearts to anything earthly — we will leave
all that is here behind us; good deeds alone go with us into the
other world. It will be wonderful to live in paradise with God,
but may God save us from hell! One must feed the soul more than
the body and pray more often, weeping over one's own sins and also
over the sins of those nearest one. Without this, not a single
human being will be saved. Many have become unbelievers today
and many have left Christ's flock. Woe unto them. For our
Shepherd is the Lord and all of His sheep go after Him, following
His teaching and fulfilling His words. It is true, there are ill and
weak sheep, those that sin, but still, they trail along behind the
flock. But faith has been lost by those who have fallen completely
behind and are left to be eaten by beasts. They left Christ's flock
and they do not listen to His voice for 'My sheep hear My voice
and I know them and they come unto me.' But to the others He
will say, 'I don't know you, go away' on His dread judgement day."

In 1897, the well-known wanderer, Ivan Ivanovich Troitsky,[5]
demised. Not long before the death of Feofil, he had spent an

entire summer at Kitayev and remembered the Blessed One with great love and emotion.

"We spent very little time in his cell," related Troitsky to Vladimir Bobkov, a monk of the Kievo-Pecherskaya Lavra. "We spent far more time in the woods. There, the Starets would have me read the Psalter aloud and from time to time he would stop me to explain it. When I would become weary, he would send me to the Goloseyevo yard for some milk which the dairy-maids were always glad to provide and which we would sip in the woods. After arriving home, the Starets would receive visitors and I prepared dumplings which were offered to all who came to him."

Here are the impressions of Starets Feofil which Troitsky conveyed in his letters to the ascetic, Starets Adrian, of the Yougskaya Dosifeyevaya Hermitage:

"The Lord gave me the honour of serving Starets Feofil even a little. One look at the physically exhausted lover of God with his strange, incomprehensible mind, at his life which he led as a true, friendless exile from some high and brilliant world, was enough to force my sleeping mind to awaken and stand in awe. I hope to relate the details of his life and my relationship with him, for the brief period, and his edifying parables, remarks, and lessons when I see you personally. It was sad to part with him. At first he wanted me to remain until the Protection Feast and later, he even wanted me to spend the winter in Kiev and recommended that I petition the Vladika of Tver for a passport for an additional year. But my arrangements with you did not allow me to consent to his request and I wavered a great deal in my thoughts. But when I received your letter which called me to you, Starets Feofil, foreseeing the position I was in, gave his blessing when he met me and said to me, 'Now I don't need you. Go where you are being called.' I was shaken by his marvellous forevision."

A much honoured nurse who had participated in the Turkish campaign, Alexandra Grigorievna Chernikova, related the following:

"I remember it as if it had just occurred. We came to Goloseyevo as a group. My mother knew Feofil very well and was quite close to him. She wanted very much to receive his blessing during this visit. The Starets was not in his cell when we came to see him and we set out to find him in the woods. I was six years old at the time and my little brother Shura was five. While we were romping around and playing, I saw a gigantic hollow oak above the precipice of a steep bank. We ran to it, looking inside, and saw a monk praying there. On his head was a cap of the type with which St. Serafim is now depicted and in his hands was an open book. I did not become frightened, but ran to our group, calling, 'Come here! Father Feofil is here!' The Starets saw that we were approaching and he came out to meet us. His face was so bright and clear and on his lips a blessed smile flickered. He blessed us children first of all. He went to Shura and said:

'You are a good child — meek, kind, and obedient. May the Lord bless you. But God also needs the good ones.'

Then he stood before me, placed his hands on my head, patted it, and sighed very deeply.

'You poor, poor child. Bitter is your fate, for all your life you will toil on earth and receive thanks from no-one.'

And what happened? Shura became ill soon after and in three months he died. I have been suffering alone all my life, using up my strength for other people and receiving no gratitude from anyone.

But this is not all. My sister, Pelagia Grigorievna Yanovskaya, went up to him and the Starets chastised her:

'See how many people you have brought, silly! If only two had come, but you have brought seventeen for blessing, thinking to take the starets away from his prayers. Take them back now if you are so clever, through this pit.'

And with this, he pointed to the big precipice.

We stood still, not understanding. 'If we go through the pit (so the older ones thought), it is marshy and muddy. Our shoes will get dirty and the children may catch cold.' So, as soon as the Starets had returned to the tree and began praying, we went back on the dry land.

Soon after this my mother, Agafiya Ivanovna Chernikova, together with a Kievan merchant's wife, Kseniya Ivanovna Mizernikova, set out to see the Blessed Starets. This time he was at home. He had high esteem for my mother and he seated her on a little bench and, turning to the merchant's wife, he said:

'Well, Kseniya Ivanovna, as soon as you return home, make me some dumplings with cabbage. But see that they are tasty. I'll send my cell-mate, Ivan, for them and you can give them to him.'

When they returned home, Mizernikova said to Mama:

'For heaven's sake, fulfil Father Feofil's request.'

'But what about you? He had asked you.'

'Actually, I don't have the time. I'll send you both butter and flour and you will have only the work to do."

Mama agreed and prepared them. On the appointed day, the cell-mate, Ivan, came and brought a huge, beautiful, soft Easter bread and two prosphora, one large and one small.

'Why did you bring prosphora, Ivan?' asked my mother.

'Batiuska Feofil sent them,' answered Ivan. 'He told me to give the widow (Mama) the Easter bread and the large prosphora and to give the merchant's wife the smaller one. The widow troubled herself and made dumplings for me, while the merchant's wife did not want to put herself to any trouble, thinking that she could fool me, an old man. So, give her the small prosphora.'

And the visionary always knew who had troubled themselves most for him."

"I was twelve years old when I first thought of going to Starets Feofil for advice," related a Kievan woman, Evfrosiniya Mikhailovna Tsybulskaya. "I was left an orphan and lived with strangers, in great want and grief. I was offended and oppressed. But having heard from good people that a 'holy batiushka' was living at Kitayev, I decided to see him, no matter what, and tell him of my grief. I didn't go alone. There were two women with me. As we were going through the woods, we met a tall, ragged monk.

'Whom are you looking for?' he asked, walking up to me.

'For Father Feofil,' I replied to him.

'Well, if you have need of him, go to his cell,' the monk said.

Along the way I wept bitterly, but my companions roared with laughter over the appearance of the starets. I was seized with annoyance that they were laughing at a man of God. 'You are silly,' I said, 'and both of you will often shed tears because of the righteous one.'

We had no sooner come to Feofil's cell than we saw that same starets coming behind us. He did not say a word to us but only looked sternly at my companions and went into his cell. In a minute he brought me a prosphora but to my companions he gave potato peelings and a dead crayfish which meant a great shame for their shameless, dissipated way of life.

'Batiushka, I want to enter the Rzhishchevsky Monastery,' I tearfully said to the Starets while accepting the prosphora.

'No!' the Starets said firmly. 'You will not live in a monastery. Near one, yes, but you will not enter it.'

'Why not, Batiushka?' I asked.

'Why? Because, until the sixty-sixth year, you will weep but in forty-eight years God will send a priest who will save you.'

I did not understand his words at that time but, in fact, a terrible misfortune did befall me. When I was eighteen, I became afflicted with a black illness and I wept dreadfully. It is a terrible, torturous illness. At first, I would be fine and well all week, working and toiling but as soon as Sunday or a feast day arrived, then the misfortune would arise. Right from morning something would begin to stick in my throat as if to choke me and my stomach would burn like fire, as if unclean spirits had taken command, and I would cry with all my strength. I tried everything and took all manner of medicines. The only relief I received was when I would run to the Great Lavra Church and come before the miraculous icon. For a while, I would feel better, but hardly would the blessing of the bread or the Cherubic Hymn begin, when I would be seized again and it would burn so terribly that I would have killed myself with a knife if only I had more strength left. I would run outside and run around the Lavra, crying at the top of my voice from the pain. It continued that way for forty-eight years, just the length of time that Starets Feofil said it would.

Finally, one day I was in the Lavra, hurrying to church, weeping as usual, when an old, grey-haired priest came up to me.

'What are you weeping about, you unfortunate creature?'

I stopped and told him about my terrible grief.

'Well, don't weep,' he told me. 'The Lord is merciful. Come closer and open your collar.'

I did so and he tied my neck tightly with a lace and then removed an icon of St. Dimitry of Rostov from his chest, hung it on my neck, looked at me compassionately, gave me his blessing and walked away saying:

'Pray, servant of God, pray fervently!'

A week went by and a feast came up. I was certain that I would have another seizure but no, nothing happened. I went to church and waited. The Cherubic Hymn was sung — nothing. The 'I Believe' and 'Our Father' — still nothing. The liturgy ended and I returned home — nothing. The illness had vanished as if it had never been at all. I ran to the Great Church and fell on my knees before the icon of St. Dimitry of Rostov and began to thank him with tears of gratitude.

Why didn't I turn to Father Feofil for help? I did, and asked for his holy prayers. He would comfort me, give me a prosphora and send me home saying, 'Go and have patience. This is fated for you. For these sufferings angels in heaven will weave you a crown.'

I lived with my sister in Pechersk at that time and we worked as launderesses. Our poverty was unbelievable. To make matters worse, my sister began to lose her eyesight and could not work. If it were not for Starets Feofil, believe me, I would have taken my own life in my youth. He was like a guardian angel, guiding and comforting us. Sometimes he would send his sister, who lived in the Florovsky Monastery as a postulant, to visit us with a prosphora. He would order her to see that we rose in time for matins every morning and once he came himself. When he arrived, we were already up and preparing to go to church. He praised us for our diligence, saying, 'That's right, toil my children. Pray and don't be lazy.'

One time he brought my little sister Dunya a little bag of peas and said, 'Go to the monastery, Dunyasha, to bake prosphora. If you listen to me, your eyes will be healed, but if you don't listen, your eyes will be like these peas.'

'Oh Batiushka, how can I go to the monastery? It would be better if you would bless me to live with my sister.'

'That means that you do not want to go to the monastery? Well then, here is my blessing to you but you will walk in darkness until your death.'

And so it happened. After this Dunya became completely blind and I have now been living near the Lavra for fifty-five years, and was possessed by demons for forty-eight years. It has now been twelve years since I was cured."

October, 1853, came. The time of going to the Lord was already approaching for the Blessed Starets. Foreseeing this, Feofil stopped taking food for exactly one month before his demise and was satisfied with only a little piece of blessed bread dipped in wine diluted with water. His feet began to swell from standing so long at prayer, but he did not pay the slightest attention to this and he redoubled his podvig of prayer. When Russia was experiencing heavy trials at the beginning of the Crimean campaign, one could notice Feofil's special striving in prayer.

Before the arrival of every sad bulletin from the theatre of war, the Starets would walk about with his head lowered and he wept unconsolably for days. Once, wishing to inform the brothers of a very unfortunate and bloody battle, he wounded his face and hands with black thorns and lay down bleeding under the overhanging eaves of the shed.

"My God what has happened to you, Batiushka?" cried the frightened Abbess Agnia who had come by chance to Kitayev.

"Nothing, nothing, my dear one. I have put one hundred leeches on my sinful body. Go! Go!"

"Good heavens! Why, Batiushka?"

"It is necessary. This is my sacrifice. A sacrifice for the Russian troops who will give their lives tonight on the battlefield for faith, Tsar, and fatherland."

But regardless of causing such torments to his body and of his great loss of strength, the Starets continued to attend the liturgy, matins and vespers as before. He partook of the Holy Mysteries of Christ almost every day, read the rules of the holy fathers, prostrated endlessly, read the Psalter and Gospel, and instructed pilgrims. At the end of winter, the Blessed One became worthy of the revelation of the time of his imminent departure and he called his cell-mate, Ivan, to himself and said:

"Ivan, what are you thinking about at this moment?"

"I'm not thinking of anything," he replied.

"And I am thinking of petitioning the Heavenly King to allow me to spend this winter on earth because Praskoviya [that was his way of calling the Holy Martyr, Paraskeva, whom he especially honoured] does not want to dig a grave for me in winter."

Ivan did not pay attention to these words until the demise of the Starets took place.

The second time, the Starets called his other cell-mate, Panteleimon, to the window of his cell and said, pointing to the monastery yard:

"Look, Panteleimon, there is a cross above the grave. Do you see it?"

"No, I don't," the cell-mate replied because, in truth, there was neither cross nor grave in the place to where Father Feofil was pointing and only after the demise of the Blessed Starets, when the cell-mate returned to Kiev from a pilgrimage, did he see the grave of the Blessed One, with a cross erected by his spiritual children, in that very spot which Feofil had pointed out.

A week before his demise, the Starets asked the Kitayevskaya postulants to bring earth from the Dniepr and pour it near his cell in the form of a grave. Then he measured its length and width with a stick and afterwards would not part with the stick.

"I should have died a long time ago," he used to repeat, "but Praskoviya is praying to God for me."

The cell-mate, Ivan, seeing that the Starets was not jesting about the nearness of his death, began to grieve and to be sad about his future fate.

"Batiushka," he wept, "to whom will you leave us? For God's sake, ask the deputy of the Lavra to enter me into the number of the brotherhood."

"They will enter you and not only that, but they will also make you a monk."

"Who? Me? An indecent servant? A former fugitive and tramp? Oh no! That would never happen. No!"

"In little faith you came to me, but the Lord will place you above many," the Blessed One replied to him.

On that same day, the Starets went to the deputy of the Lavra, Archimandrite Ioann, told him something unusual about Ivan, after which the deputy joyfully agreed to the tonsuring of the cell-mate to the monkhood and gave him the name of Dmitry.

After his tonsure, the Lavra brothers began asking Dmitry about the reason for his sudden tonsure to the monkhood, but the cell-mate replied:

"I cannot tell you. It is a secret. Only Starets Feofil, the deputy, and I know about it. If I tell about it, then, according to the words of Starets Feofil, the deputy and I will immediately die."

The Starets extended his protection to many others besides Dmitry. He personally interceded for his sister, the Florovsky postulant Anna, and was present at her tonsuring not long before his demise. Moreover, the Starets had many spiritual children in the city and he would visit them daily, giving them comfort and strengthening them with prayer. He gave them his final instructions and carried out many charitable deeds.

One eye-witness related the following astonishing event:

"In Shulyavka, on the outskirts of Kiev, there lived a poor widow named Rudnichikha and her daughter. While her husband was alive, they had lived comfortably and well. They maintained post-horses and were engaged in business but, on becoming a widow, Rudnichikha was left without any means and fell into extreme poverty. She lived her lonely life with great effort and toil and was often without bread. Then, to complete her misfortune, her daughter took to her bed with a fatal illness. It was quite late at night and the girl was lying unconscious. The mother's heart was torn with despair. The last minutes of the dying girl were approaching and there could be no help. 'Oh God, how wretched I am,' sobbed the desperate mother. 'Everyone has abandoned me, poor and penniless that I am. If only I could go to Batiushka Feofil for advice. If only I could pour out my grief to him and ask him for his holy prayers for my beloved daughter.' But it was many versts to the Kitayevskaya Hermitage and she could not leave the side of her dying daughter.

Suddenly, it seemed to the mother as if someone had walked past the window and come into the porch. 'Who could this be as such a late hour?' Rudnichikha thought as she went to the door, but when she opened it, she was left dumbfounded. There stood Starets Feofil, looking at her with great tenderness. 'Peace be unto you. Don't be afraid, it is I. You wanted to see me and so I have come to you.' He went straight to the bed and blessed the little one. Rudnichikha fell at his feet and wept loudly. 'Quiet, don't weep,' the Starets comforted her. 'Your daughter is not dying. She is only cold.' He removed his warm outer cloak, covered the girl with it and began to pray. After half an hour, he put his cloak back on and silently left the hut. The troubled mother came to the bed of her dying daughter, but the girl was already looking around with a joyous smile. 'Mama! I feel so much better now. But who was just here?' 'Father Feofil, my dear one,' replied the rejoicing mother. 'Father Feofil? Why didn't you wake me up?' 'But you were near death, my child.' The girl got out of the bed and walked about the room. Within an hour she was completely restored to health to the great amazement of the neighbors."

There were three days left of the earthly life of God's Starets. There arose some sort of special activity within Feofil. He gave various orders, the meanings of which were understandable only to him. For example, he placed a bench across the threshold of his cell and lay down upon it. He told his cell-mate that for the first time in thirty-eight years he was lying so peacefully and that he was amazed that he had not thought of it before. Then, he called Dmitry over to himself and gave him some incense and myrrh, ordering him to take it quickly to the deputy, Ioann. This was on Monday, October 26, and by the time the cell-mate got to the Lavra, matins had already begun there. The deputy was standing in the altar of the Great Church at this time and when Dmitry handed him the incense and myrrh, he was quite startled. With unbearable curiosity, he set out for Kitayev to visit the Blessed One immediately after matins.

"Father Feofil, why did you send me incense and myrrh?" asked Ioann, hurriedly entering into the cell.

"On Wednesday we shall be burying..."

"Whom?"

"Him whom God calls. Perhaps even me."

"You? The Lord be with you. What are you saying?"

"The waves of death encompass me and the snares of death prevented me" (2 Samuel 22:5; Psalm 18:5).

"If you are really preparing to leave us forever, I shall order a coffin for you. Which would you prefer, pine or oak?"

"None is necessary. It has long been ready."

"Where is it?"

"It is lying in the belfry."

Someone was sent to the belfry and, indeed, a long box, similar to a coffin, was found there. The church candles had once been stored in it and its cover was on hinges as with a trunk lid.

"Do you mean that you are to be buried in this?" the deputy asked dubiously.

"In it, my teacher. That is my will. Amen."

After the deputy had departed, the Starets sent a messenger to the superior of the hermitage, Hieromonk Anatoly, with the request that on Wednesday, October 28, he would be brought the Holy Gifts to his cell. He repeated this several times, adding that it was to be the last time. The Starets' desire was fulfilled. He received the Holy Mysteries early in the morning and became completely at peace.

Before vespers, he sent one of his cell-mates to the market place to buy three rolls of bread, incense, and honey, and to Dmitry he said:

"Don't leave the cell today and you will see something extraordinary."

Then he requested that the cell be cleaned of all rubbish and swept up, saying that he must be received in a Christian manner. Then he asked his cell-mate to light the stove, to place some incense and myrrh on coals in a pan and to light the votive lamp before the icons. When Dmitry said it was still early and that the bells had not yet rung for vespers, Feofil said:

"This time it is necessary. Fulfill the obedience to the end."

The lamp was lighted.

"That's right. Now it's good. Make certain that it does not go out."

Then he lay on the bench which he had placed across the threshold of his cell, with his head in the entrance hall. He asked that two wax candles be lighted and stuck to the door posts and that he be given the cross with which he used to bless those who came to him and, having blessed his cell-mates with this cross, he sent one of them to the superior of the hermitage, Hieromonk Anatoly, with the order to inform him that "Feofil has demised; toll the bell." The cell-mate obeyed and related the Starets' words to Anatoly. In the heat of the moment, Father Anatoly did not comprehend all that was said and hurried to send the bell-ringer to the belfry to inform the brotherhood of the repose of the Righteous One. But suddenly, he thought of something and asked:

"Who did you say sent you to me?"

"Batiushka Feofil."

"That means that he uttered this request with his own lips?"

"His own. . . "

"Then how do you know that he has already died?"

And he hurried to the cell of the Blessed One to find out what had happened to him.

Meanwhile, Dmitry was left alone in the cell and, not knowing what to do, began to adjust the candles so that they would not burn the lintel. He did not leave the head of the bench upon which the dying Starets lay and he quietly wept. It was difficult for him to face the impending separation from his beloved spiritual father under whose prayerful wing he had lived so warmly. He stood silently, with lowered head, at the death bed, listening to the last instructions of his dear teacher and he broke into loud sobs, endlessly kissing his hands. Suddenly, something flashed before his gaze and a current of cool air struck his face. Dmitry looked upwards in amazement and became petrified. In the cell, the ceiling began to rise and the blue sky, as if extending its arms, was preparing to receive the holy soul of the dying Righteous One.

"O Lord, into Thy hands I yield my spirit," said the dying

Starets, in a scarcely audible whisper and in an instant, inexorable death forever closed his God-praising lips.

Dmitry could not control himself but began to tremble and with a loud cry of desperate amazement, he ran, in fear, into the courtyard. While running through the monastery gate, he collided with the superior, Father Anatoly, and the other cell-mate who were on their way to the cell of the Blessed One to see what had happened.

When they entered the cell, everything was as it had been before. The ceiling had descended and was resting in its proper place. Starets Feofil was lying motionless on the bench, his emaciated hands folded on his breast. The face of the deceased Righteous One shone with heavenly grace and death could not place its gloomy stamp on the grace-adorned face of the Blessed Starets. No sooner had he released his last breath than an undefinable fragrance filled the cell. Thus, he yielded up his life quietly and at peace and handed over his righteous soul into the hands of God on October 28, 1853, on the feast Day of the Nun-Martyr, Paraskeva, who is called Pyatnitsa, at five o'clock in the afternoon.

News of the repose of the Blessed Feofil brought great crowds of people to the Kitayevskaya Hermitage, not only from Kiev and the outlying settlements, but also from other cities in the region. The dense crowd surrounded the coffin of the deceased Starets in a tight ring and the walls of the Kitayevskaya Church resounded with the uninterrupted singing of services for the repose of his righteous, much-suffering soul. Each person wanted to pay his last respects to the departed and to touch, if not his body, then at least his coffin or to take as a remembrance and blessing something from his garments or from his cell. And the coffin of the Starets was completely covered with wax candles which were stuck to the sides by his numerous followers.

Few people wept. Everyone stood with calm faces, breaking the pious silence only with deep sighs of contrition about their endless sins.

"It is not with weeping that we bid farewell at the death of the holy ones," says St. Basil the Great, "but in triumphant praising we rejoice at their coffins, because, for the righteous, death is a sleep or, rather to say, their departure is to a better life." Thus it was here. Each person consciously felt that, although the Starets had demised, although he had left for the Heavenly

Father, he did not take away with him the love for the living. Although he passed away in body, in spirit he remained on earth with those true to him.

"Stop, behold, and learn!" the unbreathing body of the Blessed Starets Feofil advised those surrounding it. "Leave the vanity of this world for its wells are useless, they cannot hold within themselves saving water. Yesterday, my eyes saw, my ears heard, my lips spoke, and my body moved. But the spirit of life has left it and what is now before you? And so remember, my friend, to live in fear for all our earthly life is nothing but a daily death. Yesterday, we were not as we are today. Tomorrow we will not be as today. Each day, a part of our life vanishes and at the very time when we are growing, life is receding and diminishing. Your brother has died today and tomorrow you will die. The route is the same for all. All the earth is sown with bones of the deceased like a field of wheat and the living cannot find a spot upon which to step without disturbing with their feet the remains of the deceased. Do not seek delights for sight and hearing, for tomorrow your eyes will close and your ears will stop hearing. Do not give will to your hands and feet. Tomorrow the hand of death will bind them and you yourself will be welded to your death-bed from which you will rise. Do not desire splendid clothing or grand houses, for tomorrow you will be clothed in a shroud and a coffin will be your house. Do not desire rewards and distinction, for they will be displayed only temporarily near your coffin, as if laughing at your vainglory. Do not tie yourself down to the earth or to anything earthly, for tomorrow the scythe of death will sever all such ties and against your will and desire, you will go to the distant country of another world where everything is different and will remind you of nothing of your earthly riches and treasures. Keep vigil and hurry to settle over there in good time in thought and heart so that at that hour when you are led to this region, you will not find yourself in a strange place, unfamiliar with the order there."

In accordance with the orders of the departed Starets, his emaciated body was garbed in his schema and placed in that old coffin in which he had asked to be buried. The burial was ceremoniously carried out by the deputy of the Lavra, Archimandrite Ioann (who later became Bishop of Poltava), together with the superior of the hermitage, Hieromonk Anatoly and many startsy, with the participation of the kliros singers of the Lavra under the direction of the regulator, Hieromonk Modest. The Holy Trinity Church and the entire monastery yard were full of worshippers. Before the beginning of the last kissing, the deputy of the Lavra gave a touching, deeply edifying oration and upon completing it, the coffin, with the dear remains of the reposed Righteous One, the beloved spiritual father of all, was carried from the church into the monastery yard. The weather on that day was wonderful — warm, quiet, sunny, and bright. There was not the least breeze in the air and the wax candles in the hands of the worshippers burned brightly with peaceful flames as if testifying that the soul of the deceased Starets, like a bright, unflickering candle, was now standing before the face of Vladika, the Lord Himself. The funeral procession was made around the Holy Trinity Church, preceded by banner-bearers, and the Holy Gospel. Then the coffin was lowered into the bowels of the earth while the bells of the Kitayevskaya Hermitage tolled and "Holy God" was sung.

The grave of Hieroschemamonk Feofil, fool-for-Christ's-sake, is located in the Kitayevskaya Hermitage near the Holy Trinity Church on the northern side next to the grave of the Kievo-Lavra eremite Dosifei. On its tombstone are inscribed the following words:

"Here lie the remains of Hieroschemamonk Feofil who was tonsured into monkhood in the Kievo-Bratsky Bogoyavlensky Monastery in 1821, on December 11; ordained hierodeacon on September 30, 1822; ordained hieromonk on January 6, 1827;[6] tonsured into the schema on December 9, 1834, there (at the Kievo-Bratsky Monastery). And deceased in the Holy Trinity Kitayev-skaya Hermitage on October 28, 1853, in the sixty-fifth year from his birth. O Lord, settle his soul in the dwellings of the righteous and grant that his memory be eternal."

Hieroshemamonk Feofil was rather tall. His light face and bright blue eyes did not at all harmonize with the sullen countenance which he sometimes took on himself in dealing with people. He had a short, narrow beard which he did not cut but rather, he pulled hairs out of it. He spoke in a monotone and quite quickly, usually using the Little-Russian dialect. No-one ever saw him laughing, but often weeping and these constant tears, like expensive beads, served as atonement before the eyes of the Lord for the multitude of our sins.

The memory of Blessed Feofil's God-pleasing life and wonderful deeds did not cease with his demise. He is still quick and incessant in giving help in illness and grief to all who call to him. This is eloquently witnessed to by the numerous panikhidas which are still sung at the grave of the deceased Rightous One at the request of various people who come from the remotest corners of Russia. Many of the sick and afflicted, for whom human help was powerless, were convinced in dreams to turn to Blessed Feofil in their prayers and through their faith, they were worthy to receive healing.

Here are only two of the many incidents which were related to the compiler:

1. A Greek doctor from Jerusalem suffered from gout and was confined to a wheelchair for several years and he had no hopes of recovering. Once, Starets Feofil appeared to him in a dream and said:

"Go to Kiev, pay reverence to the saints and then go to the Kitayevskaya Hermitage and have a Panikhida served at my grave and you will be healed. I am Hieroschemamonk Feofil."

The Greek paid no attention to the dream, but on the following night, the same thing occurred. On the third night Feofil appeared and sternly demanded that his directions be fulfilled. The doctor awoke in fear and gave his oath to make the journey. He immediately felt a certain easing so that he could already walk on crutches instead of using his wheelchair.

He arrived in Kiev in 1882, accompanied by his wife, but not knowing the Russian language, he turned to Metropolitan Platon for aid. The Metropolitan directed him to Kitayev and told him to have a panikhida served at the grave of Starets Feofil.

The doctor complied with this, then venerated the relics of the holy saints of the Lavra and left for home completely cured.

2. Matfei Vasilievich Kocherzhinsky, a native of the Kiev-Podol province, related the following details in a dream:

"In 186? I entered the M - - Monastery. At that time I was still a young lad and my heart was filled with strong zealousness for monastic podvigs and toils, but I was without the guidance of an experienced supervisor-starets and it was very difficult for me to reach my goal. I was very much grieved in spirit about this, being carried away in thought to the days of the ancient desert life when each beginning monk had his own experienced starets-instructor. Having prayed fervently, I decided to give myself up to God's will and the Lord heard me.

One night while I was in my cell sleeping serenely, a tall, old schemamonk appeared before me. He had a cane in his hand and, walking up to my bed, he said:

'Is this how you are conquering your lascivious passions, Matfei? Is this how you are preparing to be Christ's warrior? Is this how you are starting your salvation? No, that is not the way, not like that! This is how ... ' And with these words, he threw my quilt onto the floor, then my pillow and my sheet and so on. I awoke in confusion. Beads of perspiration ran down my brow. My feet and arms were trembling. My heart trembled and beat rapidly.

'My God, who is it? Where am I?' I thought crossing myself. In the morning I gave my bed away to the needy and decided, from that day on, to sleep on the bare floor, placing a small roll of felt under my head. Some time passed but the stern starets did not leave my mind. Whether I was working or just walking, his accusations weighed on my soul. I once encountered one of the young monks, Pavel, the candle-maker, who was very friendly towards me. He asked me to visit him for a cup of tea and when I arrived, we sat down to converse. Suddenly my gaze, which had been roaming over the walls, stopped on the portrait of an old starets and having taken a good look at it, I became dumbfounded.

'It is he!!' my lips whispered. 'Yes, he! This is the very same starets who appeared to me in a dream — who is he?'

The master of the cell quickly explained about the portrait of Blessed Feofil and in a minute, I was kissing the portrait with grateful lips. Soon, I had a copy made which hangs in my cell above my sleeping place and there it will hang until the end of my life as an obvious, graphic accuser of human whims and passions and a constant witness that man needs very little while he is on earth."

With those words, my interlocutor brought out the portrait of Blessed Feofil and we sank into deep, silent contemplation."

FOOTNOTES

[1] The sources of all the examples and cases related in this book are:
   a) Honoured older residents of Kiev.
   b) From experiences related by the cell-mates of the Blessed Starets.
   c) Gavrily Feodorovich Galushka (later monk Platon), the former valet of Metropolitan Filaret.
   d) Numerous stories told by the monks and nuns of the Kievo-Pecherskaya Lavra, the Mikhailovsky and Florovsky Monasteries, assured by their priestly and monastic consciences.
   e) The honoured nurse, Alexandra Grigorievna Chernikova, a participant in the Turkish campaign and a lifelong friend of the Blessed One.

[2] Abbess Agnia was born Anna Grindling. She was converted to Orthodoxy from the Lutheran sect and became a postulant at the Florovsky Monastery in 1829. She was endowed with an extraordinary meekness of spirit and a loving heart for which she was especially loved by the Blessed Starets. In 1850, Feofil tonsured her to the schema with the name of Barbara but she kept this secret until her death on September 30, 1865.

[3] Emperor Nikolai Pavlovich visited Kiev fifteen times and was in the Lavra about thirty times.

He visited Kiev for the first time in 1816 while still a Grand Duke.

The second visit took place on June 23-26, 1829, after he had become Tsar.

The third visit was on May 31 to June 2, 1830.

The fourth, in September, 1832.

The fifth, on September 10-11, 1835.

During his sixth visit, which occurred on August 14-16, 1837, His Majesty, in accordance with a promise to Metropolitan Filaret, attended the liturgy celebrating the feast day of the Lavra, The Repose of the Theotokos (August 15). After the liturgy, the Tsar proceeded to the Metropolitan's chambers for a visit. While crossing the Lavra courtyard, he noticed the customary dinner being given out to the poor and the pilgrims. This custom, which was observed each year, had been established by the founders of the Lavra, Sts. Antony and Feodosy, and was maintained according to their will. Having been told the details of this event, His Majesty wished to try the food which was being distributed to the people. They brought him a wooden plate and a wooden spoon with bread, sour cabbage soup and millet gruel with milk. His Majesty ate the food, praised its taste and said, "I am very pleased that the ancient customs are observed. I wish that in the future the holy traditions of our blessed fathers will be preserved in their entirety for the guidance of our contemporaries and for the instruction of posterity." The wooden utensils used by the Tsar were preserved in the Lavra Vestry in memory of his visit. His Majesty left Kiev on August 16.

The seventh visit took place from August 10 to 12, 1840.

The eighth, on September 19, 1848.

He arrived for the ninth time on May 21, 1845, accompanied by the Grand Duke Konstantin Konstantinovich and the following day of the Ascension, he was at the Sofia Cathedral for the liturgy. Later, he visited the Lavra. Since His Majesty's arrival was unannounced, it threw the brotherhood into a great bustle. The monks were in the refectory at the time and when His Majesty's arrival became known, all began to rush about. Some spread rugs, others put on robes, while still others lighted candles. But His Majesty had gone into the church. He looked around and saw no-one but an old man lighting the chandelier. His Majesty touched the old man on the elbow and said, "Leave it; it is not necessary." The monk did not turn around, assuming that one of the postulants, who did not know of the Tsar's arrival, was speaking to him. He pushed the Sovereign with his elbow and angrily retorted, "No-one is asking you. Go away! I know myself what is necessary." His Majesty smiled and went on his way. The old man was horrified when he was later told that his sharp reply had been made to the Tsar. Having venerated the holy icons and relics, His Majesty received the Metropolitan's blessing and left for St. Petersburg.

The tenth time His Majesty was in Kiev and at the Lavra for a total of seven hours since he was only passing through.

On September 8, 1847, His Majesty made his eleventh arrival in Kiev. He was expected to arrive at 6 P.M., but for some reason he arrived at 6 A.M. Nikolai Pavlovich rode up to the Holy Lavra gates, left the carriage and set out for the Great Church accompanied by his Adjutant-General, Orlov. The doors of the church were still closed because of the early hour. The wide Lavra courtyard and especially the threshold of the church were filled with sleeping pilgrims who had gathered here for the forthcoming feastday of the Birth of the Theotokos. His Majesty stopped before the church, examined the depictions of the saints at the entrance of the church and read the troparion and kondakion of the church's feast (The Repose of the Theotokos) inscribed in gold letters on both sides of the church doors. Soon a monk appeared in the courtyard. His Majesty called him over and inquired about the times of the services in the Lavra Chuch and asked that the doors be opened. Entering the church, as usual, His Majesty venerated the holy relics and icons and was ready to leave when the deputy of the Lavra, Archimandrite Lavrenty, appeared and escorted His Majesty to the gates. Because of the early hour of his arrival and departure, almost no-one noticed His Majesty, neither the monastery brethren, nor the inhabitants of Pechersk.

His Majesty's twelfth visit occurred on September 21, 1850. On Sunday, September 24, Nikolai Pavlovich attended the liturgy in the Lavra which was served by the Metropolitan. At the end of the service, His Majesty spoke with Filaret and mentioned, in the conversation, "Your service was beautiful. Only tell the deacons not to yell." It must be noted that at that time, the senior deacon in the Lavra was Antony. His voice was thunderous but somewhat sharp. It was once joked that his singing of "Many Years" could be heard all the way to Belaya Tserkov. Of course, in the Tsar's presence, Antony tried especially hard to distinguish himself with his voice, but its harsh timbre, as we have seen, did not appeal to His Majesty. In order to prevent a repetition of the incident, the Metropolitan issued the following order to the Ecclesiastical Sobor of the Lavra: "His Majesty the Emperor who was present during the serving of the divine liturgy on September 24, deigned to express a most gracious approval of the service. At the same time, His Majesty, having noticed the highly unpleasant shouting of the senior deacon, Antony, deigned to order me to restrain deacons in general from the excessive raising of voices during services." The Ecclesiastical Sobor hastened to implement this order. On September 25, at 10:30 A.M., His Majesty left Kiev ... and etc. (Archives of the Kievo-Pecherskaya Lavra; Matters concerning High-Ranking Visits)

[4] The finding of this icon occured in the 1840's under the following circumstances:

An ill peasant woman from Voronezh province arrived at the Lavra and stated that the Mother of God had appeared to her in a dream and ordered her to go to the Lavra to find the "Chenstokhovskaya" icon of herself which would be found in oblivion in the bread-house. "If you have a molieben served before the icon, then you will be cured," said the Queen of Heaven. On the persistent requests of the woman, the Lavra monks made a careful search and, indeed, amongst some old things preserved in the store-room, the icon was found. The ill woman immediately had a molieben served before it and went home completely recovered. From that time, the icon was placed, with honour, on the wall and many cures were granted to those who came to her with faith. A child from the town of Kotelva in Kharkov province, Gregory Krivusha, suffered from tormenting rheumatism for five years. His father vowed to have an expensive silver mounting made for the icon if his child was healed. The child was cured and the grateful father ordered an expensive silver mounting from Moscow for the icon in 1887 and had Archimandrite Levky and the monk Amfilokhy construct an expensive gilded, carved icon case for it.

[5] Ivan Ivanovich Troitsky had graduated from the Tver Ecclesiastical Seminary and wandered for more than fifty years. Just before his death, he fasted and took communion at the Sophia Monastery for women in Rybinsk. Then, the ill man, accompanied by his spiritual father, went to Moscow where he stayed with strangers. The mistress of the house became concerned about the condition of his health and feared that something unfortunate might happen to him, but Ivan Ivanovich said, "Don't worry, my dear woman, because angels will be in your home for six weeks. A certain Feodor Feodorovich will come from Bezhetsk for me." After this, the ill man, disregarding his extreme weakness, went to the all-night vigil from which he was brought back unconscious. He awakened at 7 A.M. in bed and asked, "For which liturgy are they ringing the bells?" He was answered with, "For the early one, but lie until the late one and we will wake you up." The ill man fell asleep again, but he no longer woke up. Informed about the death of the starets-wanderer, the merchant Feodor Feodorovich came to Moscow and took the body to Bezhesk for burial.

[6] This conflict in date appears in the original. On page 13 the date of Feofil's ordination is given as February 6, 1827. The translators could not correct this error, not knowing which one is accurate.